History on your Doorstep

For DJW.

History on your Doorstep

by J.R.Ravensdale

Edited by Bryn Brooks

British Broadcasting Corporation

We shall not cease from exploration
And the end of all our exploring
Will be to arrive where we started
And know the place for the first time.

T. S. Eliot

This book is published in conjunction with
the BBC television series *History on your Doorstep*,
first transmitted on BBC 2 from January 1982
and produced by Bryn Brooks

Published to accompany a series of programmes
prepared in consultation with the
BBC Continuing Education Advisory Council

© J. R. Ravensdale 1982
First published 1982
Published by the British Broadcasting Corporation
35 Marylebone High Street, London W1M 4AA

Filmset and printed in England by BAS Printers Limited
Over Wallop, Hampshire
This book is set in 10/11½ Ehrhardt Monophoto
ISBN 0 563 16464 6 (paperback)
ISBN 0 563 16495 6 (hardback)

Contents

Key
Words in the Glossary are italicised the first time they appear in the text, and items in the Bibliography are marked †.

Front cover: View from St Mary's in Rye, Sussex
Back cover: Cottage in Abbots Ripton, Cambridgeshire

Preface

Whilst researching the television series and book *Discovering Your Family History*, it was soon clear that there was a close overlap between family and local history. As it happened, little local history appeared. This book, which also accompanies a television series, hopes to redress the balance.

Unlike *Discovering Your Family History* this is neither a sources book nor a do-it-yourself guide. What is offered is something of the flavour of what passes when explorers of local history meet and exchange experiences. I shall never forget Professor Hoskins showing me his favourite long house on Dartmoor, or Dr Margaret Spufford introducing me to Sister Sneezby, or Dennis Jeeps making the old photographs of Willingham live. So I am endlessly indebted to all local historians and in return offer reports of explorations into the English past – a collection of gleanings and hints which I hope will interest both the beginner and the expert.

I am most grateful to Messrs. Faber & Faber for permission to use the quotation from T. S. Eliot's *Four Quartets* on the title page and to Dr Richard Muir who brought an artist's eye and an historian's understanding to the production of so many photographs. Above all my thanks are due to my friend and editor Bryn Brooks, his Assistant Producer Sally Kirkwood, and Production Assistant Liz McDowell, effectively research assistant, welfare officer and so much more besides this, thanks to whom we survived the ordeals of production.

J. R. RAVENSDALE

Acknowledgement is due to the following for permission to reproduce illustrations: AEROFILMS LTD plates 4, 60 right, 63; PROFESSOR M. W. BERESFORD plates 60 left & centre; THE BRITISH LAND COMPANY (photo Derrick Witty) plate 33; BRYN BROOKS plates 1, 44, 87, 88; CAMBRIDGESHIRE LIBRARIES plate 9; CAMBRIDGE UNIVERSITY COLLECTION plates 3, 19, 48, 49, 50, 61, 65, 66, 68, 70, 71, 73, 76, 77; COUNTY RECORD OFFICE, CAMBRIDGE plates 51, 52; COUNTY RECORD OFFICE, TRURO, DD.RD. 1026 (Courtesy of Mrs. E. Mann) plate 78; CROWN COPYRIGHT Reproduced with permission of The Controller of HMSO plate 121; EALING LIBRARY (photos Derrick Witty) plates 29, 34, 35, 40, 41, 43, 45; ESSEX COUNTY COUNCIL plates 84, 85; DENNIS JEEPS plates 90, 110; GLC MAP COLLECTION plates 30, 31, 36, 37, 38, 39, 46; MERVYN HAIRD plate 72; A. F. KERSTING plates 67, 83; RICHARD MUIR plates 2, 6, 7, 8, 10, 11, 12, 13, 15, 17, 18, 20, 21, 53, 54, 56, 57, 59, 64, 75, 93, 94, 95, 96, 97, 98, 99, 100, 101, 102, 103, 104, 105, 112, 113, 114; ORDNANCE SURVEY plates 5, 22, 47, 69, 79; JACK RAVENSDALE plates 80, 81, 92; JOHN SHEPPERSON plate 16; EDWIN SMITH plates 86, 107; WILLIAM VAUGHAN plate 14; DERRICK WITTY plates 23, 24, 25, 26, 27, 28, 32, 42.

Front cover: PICTUREPOINT LTD; Back cover: BRITISH TOURIST AUTHORITY, LONDON

Acknowledgement is also due to: FABER & FABER LTD for extract from the poem 'Little Gidding' from *Four Quartets* by T. S. Eliot.

Illustrations by Brian Delf on pages 100, 101, 108, 115, 118, 122, 123, 124.

Maps and plans by John Gilkes on pages 11, 59, 61, 69, 74, 96.

Introduction

'. . . and gives to airy nothing
A local habitation and a name.'

The pursuit of local history has its excitements. As you hunt the past of the place where you live, and of the people who lived there, the whole neighbourhood begins to talk. Stocks and stones and trees cease to be dumb. First they ask questions; then they start to help you find the answers. I remember a lady who kept a village shop telling me about a class in local history: 'I've taken my dog for a walk up and down that road practically every day for twenty years and never saw a thing. Now it's alive and packed with interest and I'm always noticing something new.'

Some of what she saw took new meaning from documents that had been read again, probably for the first time in centuries. There was the spot where the cross had once stood, where the lord of the lesser manor had once taken his post with drawn sword and dagger to prevent the villagers from rescuing their beasts that he had wrongfully impounded.* Some of the new meaning came from learning something of the language of the landscape itself. The unevennesses in the surface of the fields on either side of her walk were indications of where the village had once stood, and slight bumps and hollows traced the outlines of the houses, yards and sheds of the peasants who lived there at the end of the Middle Ages. In the past twenty-five years, thanks chiefly to the work of Professor W. G. Hoskins, and those influenced by him, such as Professors Finberg and Beresford, and Christopher Taylor,† we have come to appreciate more than ever the contribution that visual evidence, the things we can see around us, the landscape, can make to our understanding of local history, and most history *is* local.

When launching out to discover local history, there is only one place to start, the local branch of the Public Library. By putting you in touch with what is already in print about your chosen area, the local librarian can launch you on a course that you can pursue a long way on your own resources. It is surprising how, once you have started, footnotes and references which you can follow up will carry you much further. Read everything in print that is relevant before you try archives. A generation ago the chances were high that the local Parish Chest might be richer for its own parish than the County Record Office, and might afford the student an easy link from local Library to CRO. In the last few years CRO's have grown remarkably, and the contents of most Parish Chests are pouring into them. Many Local Library collections contain much archival material, and some County Record Offices are well supplied with rare printed sources. It is not quite so easy to lay down a sequence to be followed universally, since the arrangement of Libraries and Record Offices differs from place to place. The important thing is to remember that we are taking up the time of highly skilled and trained professionals who are too delighted to help, but whose time is too precious for us to waste by using them inefficiently. We should know clearly what we want when we visit them. There is always the additional chance that the archivist or librarian may turn out to be the historian of the locality, or that they will know who is likely to help you, and will put you in touch with them.

One very elementary point is that at the start the significance of many things will be completely missed because the knowledge to interpret them will only be acquired later. This means that all information, even the apparently irrelevant should be recorded, and the method of recording should be designed for easy recall. It is as well to standardise simple things such as the size of paper and record cards you intend to use and the system of filing, soon after starting. It is worth carrying a notebook for jotting down trifles that turn up unexpectedly, but it is also advisable to transfer this to your own standard card or paper and file it. Otherwise the chaos that always lurks will take over. The amount of time that can be wasted in searching for some dimly

---

*J. R. Ravensdale 'Landbeach in 1549' in *East Anglian studies*, ed. L. M. Munby. Cambridge: Heffer, 1968.

remembered jotting, which perhaps never left the back of an old envelope, is far too expensive.

What the local historian coming to study a new area should do early, probably alongside his initial reading of material, is to examine the local landscape in as much detail as possible, walking around with maps, and supplementing this with study of aerial photographs. The local librarian may be able to help in knowing where to apply to inspect these. It is the nature of history that each new scrap of evidence gets its meaning from what has been known and understood before. The stress on visual evidence of recent years has very special help to offer local historians. They are constantly enlarging their background of historical knowledge as they go their ordinary way.

If we take the most recent census for which we may consult the Enumerator's Notebook, we can find out a lot about the people of the parish in 1881, and this will inevitably give us some information about the previous generation, because age and parish of origin were included.* But if we look at the landscape or a map of it, we are looking at the resultant of all its history. Thus the landscape is a peculiarly rich source for building up the kind of general history of the locality that we need in order to interpret the fruits of our research as they become available. The sudden illumination of the subject that comes when all the fragments of different kinds of evidence lock together, like the solution of a jigsaw puzzle, is perhaps the most exciting moment in any piece of research. One moment just another brief note is added: the next comes the realisation that the explanation is complete, and the story now flows on. All the persistence through dry places is repaid. We are no longer faced with the dead words used like tombstones to hide the buried 'Causes of the Industrial Revolution', but with what happened here to people, and how real people lived here.

When we first attempt to discover our own local history, we are probably concerned primarily with one village or town. We may also want to produce a complete history from the first footprint of early man walking on the earth, to man walking on the moon. Such an attempt could well lead to discouragement, as apparently insuperable gaps in the evidence seem to preclude the construction of a continuous narrative. At such times we may feel that all our efforts are merely filling a rag-bag of scraps. This is an illusion: the more material is collected, the faster is the process whereby each clue starts to link up with the rest.

What perhaps we need most of all in the early stages of collection is patience.

Similarly, enlarging the area of study from a single community to include something of its neighbours will add to the significance of what is known about the first; it will lead to the discovery of new material as relevant to the place of first choice as to its neighbour. The work on the first is enriched, and some of the gaps are closed.

I once had an experience which illustrates this well, when I called in at a County Record Office about a hundred miles away from the place I was studying. I had to go to the town and had heard that the CRO there had a collection of charters which might contain material relevant to my neighbouring village. In fact it proved to contain a charter authorising the digging of a ditch and planting of a hedge in 1235, dividing the common fen between my village and its neighbour.** The lay-out was described so precisely that I was not only able to explain the last piece of the parish boundary, but now could also recognise the differences between the work of Roman and of medieval canal engineers in this area. In addition I had a very rare precise medieval date for the planting of a hedge.

It is, nonetheless, important to be clear fairly early on as to the extent of the area which is to be studied, and this should be chosen so that there is sufficient documentary material, but not so much that the study will never be complete. When I was a student with the Department of English Local History at Leicester, I was at first sent to reconnoitre an area of some ten villages, and when the documents surviving proved to be prodigious, I was cut back to three, and this does commonly seem a good size.

While on the preliminary reconnaissance of my fen-edge parishes, I stumbled on a trail which would not altogether let me go, although it was outside the area on which I was to conduct my major study. It proved to be a good example of how sometimes, when luck is with us, all the evidence of different kinds links up.

*These notebooks are the originals filled in by the Enumerators as they walked round house by house.
**Wrest Park Chartulary: fol. 248d. See J. R. Ravensdale *Liable to floods*, CUP, 1974.

1 Swavesey: the Search for a Medieval Town

The pub that was not there. The day was hot and dry. The morning's search through ten Cambridgeshire villages, prospecting for earthworks, had produced very little that I had not known before. My only chance for lunch would be to try the first pub as I made my way into the tenth village, Swavesey.

Suddenly I saw the name of a side-road, Rose and Crown Road, and that surely could only mean a pub. As it happened, there was no pub, but about a hundred yards up on the left, running through an orchard, was as intriguing a set of earthworks as I could wish for. A hollow way curved through the straight rows of trees, and on either side of it were set dividing ditches which formed the outline of what looked excellent example of medieval *tofts*, enclosures in which peasants' houses had stood, and there were faint traces of so-called *house-platforms*, the low rectangular mounds that mark the ruins of so many abandoned medieval peasant houses. This hollow way swung to the edge of the orchard and

1. The starting point of the search for Swavesey's past.

2. The size and scale of the earthworks when seen from ground level inside the field are quite unexpected, and suggest that there may be substantial remains under the turf.

3. (left) This aerial photograph shows Swavesey High Street across the picture with Rose and Crown road running off the top. It also reveals what looks like a deserted medieval village in the field to the right of the farm. A hollow way runs down from the main road, and is joined lower down by at least one other street. The frontage appears to be divided up by lesser ditches so that both sides of the streets seem to be lined with house platforms. Other main features appear to adjoin the road in its lower reaches.

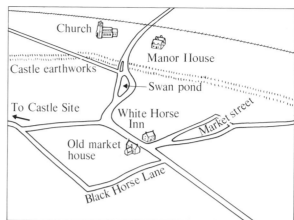

4. The aerial photograph corresponding to the OS map (plate 5) emphasises the relative emptiness of the area at the north end of the village where there is little but church, vicarage and manor house. The market is central in the picture as it must have been central in the life of the medieval village.

11

disappeared under Rose and Crown Road but re-appeared further down on the other side, swinging away on the opposite curve.

The earthworks [2] that I had stumbled on were of a pattern familiar from innumerable deserted or shrunken medieval villages, but I knew of nothing to suggest that Swavesey had ever been deserted. I needed to find more of the pattern if I could.

Air photographs rarely reveal much in the shape of earthworks in orchards, or even in fruit gardens, the trees and bushes hiding other patterns by their dominance. I went to consult archaeological air photographs of the area, but without much hope.* My pessimism was justified: nothing showed below the trees in the picture of the orchards. But across the main road, running through grass meadowland down towards the fen was another, longer, hollow way, with branches joining it, and with tofts adjacent to much of the frontage of these sunken roads [3]. The impression was confirmed that hidden beneath the present village there was the plan of an earlier Swavesey with an altogether different alignment and axis. Moreover, its heart lay remote from the heart of the modern village and even more remote from the church. Could the village have changed its site? If so, when? At this stage the landscape was posing more questions than it was answering, but the dialogue of investigation between the landscape and the observer had begun.

Swavesey today – the High Street. Swavesey immediately strikes the visitor as a big village by comparison with others in the area. It has been growing fast since the Second World War. Before the building of postwar estates, a person driving through might easily, if not quite correctly, have taken it for almost a simple street village with the church at one end, away from most of the houses. Apart from the inn on the main Cambridge–Huntingdon Road, the village does not begin for three-quarters of a mile from this old Roman Road, whereas the other end of the village nestles among the waterways. This may have something to tell us about communications as the first settlers found them and used them. They seemed to have preferred water to old roads for long-distance transport.

*Cambridge University Committee of Aerial Photography.

5. *As Local Historians will find, many of the places they investigate fall across the boundaries between two, three or four* OS *sheets. This is part of Swavesey included in the* NW *sheet of the first 6″ edition 1886.*

Is this possibly the first clue to what made Swavesey larger than its neighbours, the availability of water transport? Could it have been an inland port?

Coming in from the Roman Road, through the section of the village known as Boxworth End (Boxworth being the nearest village in that direction), houses and gardens take up most of the frontage. Many of these houses are quite old, one at least appearing to be from the seventeenth century.

The next section, Middle Watch, has more old houses. One of these, Ryder's Farm [6], may have medieval work in its middle range, but it contains a good deal of seventeenth century work at least.

The end of Middle Watch is where the High Street passes over Turnbridge [7], now a fixed stone bridge.

6. Ryder's Farm. The middle range of this farmhouse – covered by the long 'cat slide' roof suggests an aisled hall and possible medieval origins. Whether or not Ryder's Farm is so old, a good deal of the rest of the fabric appears to be from the seventeenth century.

Fifty yards along on the right Wallman's Lane slips off between buildings old and new. A few years ago the space between this and the market was closely packed with timber-framed buildings. A little further on the left is Black Horse Lane with a splendid red brick house dating from the beginning of the eighteenth century, with a schoolhouse adjoining. The properties here were all laid out in squares and rectangles, although much of this pattern has been degraded by centuries of cutting corners whenever possible, or obscured by buildings in

7. *A lesser place name packed with meaning. Turnbridge is a stone culvert, and the prolific undergrowth helps to hide the waters which once defended the town. Few visitors who pass over it connect the name with a drawbridge defending a medieval town from its main landward approach.*

8. One of the many surprises for anyone on a first visit to Swavesey is the wide market street. The old market place is now a conveniently central parking place. The Market House standing at its head on the High Street, suggests a period of prosperity in the late seventeenth or early eighteenth century that did not last.

the last few years. Not long ago the great house had a formal garden across the road from it in the shape of a square, with parterres and low box hedges. In those days it was as if Platonic geometrical forms were struggling to show themselves through very earthy wear and tear.

Market Street. A little past the entrance to Black Horse Lane on the opposite side of the road is a surprise in a village landscape, an extraordinarily wide road [8], which swells out even wider as it recedes. Nearest the High Street the surface of this Market Street is of tarmac, providing a spacious car park, a not altogether uncommon fate for medieval market places today. Beyond is a large area of smooth grass, the old Town Pond, filled in within living memory and remembered in local tradition as the dock where barges plied until the coming of the railway [9].

Looking across the High Street down the length of Market Street is the old Market House. Of red brick and handsomely decorated, it must date from the same period as the other fine house just mentioned, the very late seventeenth or very early eighteenth century. It has since been divided and altered, probably to provide more accommodation.

9. *At the end of the market is a grassy area which looks deceptively like a village green. This picture from 1933 shows more of its true nature in the remnants of one of the two ponds which used to be here. This is the last remembered dock area in the village, and the pond was filled in within living memory.*

10. *(below) Much of the history of this inn, and by implication of its village, Swavesey, appears in hints from its external appearance. The black plinth on which it stands gives away the fact that it is a timber-framed house that has been given a brick skin. The brickwork in the gable-end suggests three, or possibly four, major reconstructions. The chimney's position and the general lay-out repeat a common Cambridgeshire theme – the house, built originally as three rooms upstairs and three rooms down, with two heated rooms on the ground-floor, given increased heated accommodation by the addition of small, square gable-end chimneys. At some stage the height of the eaves has been raised to give more head-room in the bedrooms.*

The White Horse Inn. This fascinating inn [10] is on the northern corner of Market Street with High Street. Its fabric seems to epitomise something of the early modern history of the market and its changes in prosperity. At first glance it appears to have brick walls and a tile roof. The style of the windows and door suggest the early nineteenth century. However, the front door is placed a third of the way along the façade, and the main chimney is also a third of the way along the ridge, above the door. The gable at the east end tells something of a story by itself: it shows four distinct periods of alteration. The main part of the gable, down to the ground, is of a soft red brick. The front is only a skin, one brick thick. The gable end, above the red brick mentioned, shows the line of a former steep pitch, and shoulders such as are found frequently in this area when brick gables and thatched roofs came together. The final addition is where the walls have been built up to raise the eaves and give more space in the three upstairs rooms. Both gable ends show small square chimneys added in exactly the fashion common for Cambridgeshire cottages when they were divided up, as they so often were at the end of the eighteenth or the beginning of the nineteenth century, to give more heated rooms as more people were fitted in. The brick plinth helps to give the secret away even from the outside that we are looking at a timber-framed house. Its earliest form appears to have been the most common Cambridgeshire house plan from the first half of the seventeenth century, but it appears to have been modified and modernised frequently to meet the requirements of the principal inn by the side of the market and dock. In one of its phases of modernisation it was extended back along the side of the High Street to make more rooms.

Adjacent on the same side of the market is a house of similar frontage, but with gable end chimneys and tumbling-in of the brick gable ends. A thatched roof has been covered with corrugated iron. It was probably built sometime near 1700, and there may be some significance in that, of the older houses, the four most impressive near the market are of about this date. The suggestion is of a prosperity that was not maintained.

Dockland. On the opposite side of the market place is a mansard-roofed house, timber-framed and partially brick-skinned. A pair of similar cottages is reported to

11. Strangers to the fens find it difficult to envisage what ditches like these were a few centuries ago, when barges carried all heavy goods that moved in and out. The lowering of the water-table after the great draining, makes these watercourses look impossibly small, even for narrow barges. Years ago cuts from this ditch connected to the main dock by Swavesey market.

have stood within living memory down at the side of the dock, and a very small one still stands at the far end, by the little ditches that were once canals that fed the dock and carried the narrow boats to it [11]. The whole of this area from Turnbridge on through the market and docks has a different feel from the rest of the village described so far, which was much like so many small Cambridgeshire villages. The heart of Swavesey is quite different: to judge by the buildings it was once a moderately thriving commercial centre fed by what the Ordnance Survey map shows as 'Navigation Drain'. In the fens, navigation ditches or drains, when bridged, are crossed by hump-back bridges for the benefit of the man poling a narrow barge. When the railway came through Swavesey in 1847, it was not possible to send trains over a hump-back, so a new dock was provided on the far side of the railway from the village. There it is today, still called 'New Dock' on the os map, a reed-choked pool, virtually strangled at birth by its progenitor, the railway [5].

But the os gives us further information that we might never otherwise have picked up: 'Castle (Site of)'. Only ditches and very decayed earthworks are left to disappoint us when looking for the castle [12, 13]. The mound is like a miniature motte, but does not, in its present form, fit into any known pattern. The soil here is gravel, and the ramparts have been extensively robbed. It is so much easier to stand on a bank and throw gravel down into a cart, than to stand in a hole and throw it up (out of the hole) and over the side of the cart. But enough survives irregularly for us to be able to trace a good deal of the pattern of the old enclosures. There is a northern bailey that measures, according to the *Victoria County History*, 600 ft × 300 ft.*

Until very recently, scarcely any building had taken place in this area except where its houses would front on to the causeway. In the much smaller rectangle which contains the little mound, and is mapped as the site of

*vch Cambs., vol. ii, p. 41.

12. The castle mound is very small, having been extensively robbed for gravel. The ditch in the foreground connects into the main defensive ditches surrounding the bailey and old town.

13. (right) Recent clearing of the ditch has revealed how much of this corner of the bailey survives, and in spite of the lowered water table, the ditch is still a real barrier.

the castle, only one house appears in the OS first edition (1878 survey). It is still there, timber-framed and thatched. But most of the rest of this defended commercial heart of the village has been very densely developed. It is in examining the ramparts spreading from the castle that we can see the meaning of the names, 'Turnbridge' and Wallman's Lane'. The former means a drawbridge, long replaced by a permanent stone bridge over the ditch that once guarded the entrance to the fortified area. Wallman's Lane was used as the short cut to the eastern defences of the town.

Middle Watch is that portion of Swavesey beyond Turnbridge, outside the fortified settlement. Its name, and that of Wallman's Lane, probably goes back to the system of 'Watch and Ward' for local policing set up for towns by the Statute of Winchester in 1285. Middle Watch was the undefended suburb which grew up outside the town wall and gate, its only security the watchman's patrol.

14. Even in modern aerial photographs the almost circular line of trees – the perimeter of the medieval town – still dominates the view of the present village.

Just past Market Street the High Street takes a sudden turn to the right to reveal the most astonishing part of the village scene: the left-hand side of the road dips down alongside Swan Pond [15], but the path on its left goes straight and level as a stone-surfaced causeway in front of the houses to Church Bridge. The rest of the road takes the traffic past the pond on the right, separated from it by iron railings on top of a wall built to hold the road from crumbling into the pond. In the days before the Great Drainage of the Fens the pond must have filled up, as it can now in time of flood [16], to lap against the causeway which would have formed a perfect wharf at the door of the houses. The basins of the medieval dock are revealed by the 1947 flood [28].

Church End. The last section of the village, as we continue on this route from south to north along the main street, is the least built-up. To the left is a splendid church, with a Victorian vicarage behind it. Opposite is a very handsome Elizabethan house with farm buildings and an ancient-looking garden wall. Beyond is the railway halt [19].

The church is remarkable [17]. Far larger than most village churches, approached from the east it appears like two churches joined together. Inside, it appears at first as a church with two unequal aisles, but the south aisle is so large as to rival the main nave and chancel. To the north, over the churchyard wall are extensive earthworks and moats [18].

15. *One of the peculiar features of Swavesey is the way the road divides as it passes around Swan Pond, the low side against the old causeway on which the houses are built, and the other, carrying the traffic, built up to height that should clear all floods.*

16. *(right) This picture taken at the time of the Great 1947 Flood reveals the size of the causeway. High as the floods were, none of these houses was flooded. Swan Pond was obviously part of the dock system before the draining of the fens and the modern road system.*

17. Entering Swavesey churchyard from the east, the visitor gets the impression not of one but of two churches joined together side by side. The straight joint between the two and the difference in the window tracery of the 13th century Early English on the left, and the 15th century Perpendicular on the right, reveal which has been last added.

18. (right) A little water still stands, in this picture, in the ancient moat surrounding the Priory. Between this moat and the church, the earthworks suggest that there is still much to be discovered from investigating this monastic site.

19. The air photograph suggests the outline of the monastic precinct which embraced not only the field with earthworks but also the area now occupied by the Vicarage and the Manor House with its walled garden. Even the land to the right of the railway line appears once to have been within the boundary.

Reconstruction

Observation of the landscape had started hares that demanded pursuit by other kinds of evidence, and from time to time in the next few years I found the puzzles of Swavesey calling me back.

Place names. As with so many English villages, the oldest piece of evidence is in its name. For this area the authoritive work on place names is P. H. Reaney's *The place names of Cambridgeshire*. This interprets the name as meaning 'Swaef's landing-place', or just possibly 'the Swabians' landing-place'. He is interpreting the ending as derived from the Anglo-Saxon form *hyd* (hithe, dock, or landing-place) rather than the ending *-eg* (island). Unfortunately he could find no versions of the name earlier than Domesday Book, and the interpretation of Saxon place names is not too trustworthy if there are no versions from Saxon times. Domesday Book itself has three forms, Suavesheda, Swavesham and Suaveseye, leaving honours even between the rival interpretations: dock, village, island. In spite of the one he chooses, the examples that Reaney offers seem to suggest that forms meaning 'dock' are less common before the thirteenth century, when a cluster of this type crops up. Both forms seem to have lasted side by side through the Middle Ages, as if both were descriptive and could make good sense.

Thus at this stage the use of place names, no less than observation of the landscape, suggested a question rather than an answer.

Maps and air photographs. The next type of evidence used was the Ordnance Survey map. I was using mainly the first edition 6-inch map, which was easily available in a photocopy where the clearer 25-inch of the same edition was less readily obtained. But maps, especially recent ones, carry secondary historical evidence in the form of legends giving archaeological information of a kind that no air photograph can. The historical legend 'site of Priory' indicates what the earthworks north of the church are [19]. The map and air photograph together show a broad moat enclosing a large area entered by a causeway opposite the church. Platforms and more ditches suggest an extensive layout of buildings and yards. Hedges and ditches appear to outline an inner precinct as well as an outer perimeter embracing the whole of this fen island. The church is well inside both enclosures, and is related to the earthworks so intimately as to be clearly what must have been the Priory church. The road to Over is a new road shown on the Enclosure Award Map. When a sewer was put along the line of this road some years ago, it became clear that it passed through the old monks' cemetery in its proper place east of the church. Some of the stone coffins uncovered then are in the church now. The skulls that came up were placed on the garden wall of the manor house which then housed the doctor's surgery; thus patients going in had a proper medieval subject for meditation.

The church – structure. The interior of the church has also much to tell. The south-eastern corner of the nave shows Saxon 'long and short work' [20] at the *quoin*, with the kind of diagonal tooling made by dressing with an axe, common to the Saxon and early Norman periods. Until very recently, one long and one short stone, which were left unplastered, revealed the south-eastern corner of the Saxon chancel. The Saxon church so indicated was substantial for its time, quite tall, if not the full height of the church as it stands today. The width of the chancel and nave seem unchanged, but the chancel was about two-thirds of the present length, its end wall coming just a little to the east of the modern altar rail.

On to this Saxon chancel has been added a south aisle almost as wide as the main nave. Two thirteenth-century arches pierce the Saxon wall, and the mould-

20. The quoin made up of 'long and short' work, with the diagonal tooling from the stone dressing axe, shows where the south-east corner of the Saxon style church stood.

ings on the bases of the shafts suggest a date somewhere around 1275. The east window of the south aisle is also in thirteenth-century style, and in spite of very heavy restoration of the exterior, the interior looks genuine enough. There is also in the south wall of this aisle or chapel, a piece of thirteenth-century shaft [21] and arch from a *sedilia* or *piscina* in days when the floor was lower than it is today.

When this aisle was first added it would appear to have projected well beyond the old Saxon east end. The main chancel was extended to join it, as the *straight joint* in the stones outside shows. The extended chancel has a superb early fourteenth century sedilia, and its east window is from the fifteenth. Similarly, the aisle added in the thirteenth century appears to have been extended westwards in several stages, but most in the fourteenth-century, and was completed in the seventeenth century before the Civil War.

21. This fragment of the shaft from a 13th century sedilia also shows that the new chancel was added at this period.

The church – early history.

The *Victoria County History* for Cambridgeshire gives summary histories of the religious houses in the county, as was the normal practice of the editors of these volumes.* Count Alan of Brittany granted the church of Swavesey and its offerings to the Benedictine Abbey of SS Sergius and Bacchus at Angers. He had himself received it of William the Conqueror. What is strange is that there is no mention of the monastery under Swavesey in the Domesday Book, yet the prior and monks of Swavesey are mentioned as holding land in Dry Drayton. In spite of the early stonework of Saxon style in the fabric, it appears that Count Alan's grant was the effective foundation of the priory, and so it must have come between the Conquest and the Domesday survey and have been novel enough at the time of the latter to have been missed when the Commissioners were recording the manors of Swavesey.

The site of the priory when it was first founded would have been particularly attractive to Norman founders who were activated by the spirit of the monastic reforms on the Continent, because it was cut off from the evils of the world by the black waters which lapped around its walls most of the year. Here they set the Saxon masons to work, who built the only way they knew, hence this stylistic hangover after the Conquest. Count Alan must have been quick off the mark with the foundation. If the settlement of Swavesey at that period was where we found the deserted ways and houses, then the church would have been very remote indeed. If this present church was built for the priory, where was the previous parish church?

The author in the *Victoria County History* follows the argument that there never could have been a convent in any real sense at Swavesey, partly because there is no mention of 'a convent and monks serving God there' after 1272. It is also said that the first we hear of a vicar of Swavesey is very early in the fourteenth century when the later priors were also vicars of the parish.

It is hard not to believe that the wide south aisle, added to the church about the time when we first hear of a vicar, is not a parochial aisle. The man and the building match each other, the prior/vicar, and the monastic/parish church. It is also difficult to look over the churchyard wall to the north and not believe that Swavesey priory was ever a serious community. So we have found our *parish church* from the late thirteenth century onwards as the south aisle. Was there another before this in the remote, deserted settlement? We do not yet know.

In its later life the convent had difficulties. As an alien priory with its mother abbey in France, every time the two countries were at war (which was a good deal of the time in the later Middle Ages), its revenues were seized into the King's hands, and usually farmed out to the highest bidder. In 1411 it passed permanently to the Prior and Convent of St Anne at Coventry, a Carthusian house, until the Dissolution in 1539.

Printed sources.

At this stage we had only been able to get precise dates from the secondary printed sources

*VCH Cambs. vol. ii, p. 197.

that we had used, the account of the history of the priory in the *Victoria County History*. But Farrer's *Feudal Cambridgeshire*[†] has collected together medieval fragments under the parishes to which they refer. In 1230 Roger de la Zouch acquired a *manor* in Swavesey by exchange for his lands in Brittany. In 1232 he was granted fifteen oaks for making lodgings at his manor of Swavesey. In 1244 he obtained the grant of a market and fair, and the grant was enlarged in 1261. In 1267 there was a grant to Alan la Zuche, whose corn had lately been burned by the king's enemies. This was the year in which the 'Disinherited'[*] were raiding the countryside from their base in the Isle of Ely. They were desperate knights who had lost everything through their support of Simon de Montfort against King Henry III during the 'Barons' Wars'. Swavesey was one of the convents raided. Its chest was broken into among other damage, and valuables taken from it. The chest would have been the local strong safe deposit, secure against all except the most impious. These few fragments of information combine particularly well with the evidence we had found with our eyes from the landscape, the maps, and the air photographs and, above all, the church.

Lords of the manor. The de la Zouch family seems to have valued Swavesey highly. First there was the building of a residence, and then the signs of developing the settlement commercially from at least the 1240s.

The obvious book to consult at this stage was Professor Maurice Beresford's *New towns of the Middle Ages*.[†] In this the author named Cambridgeshire as the only county which had no planned new town in the Middle Ages, although he did not know why.

The disappearance of the village from whose remains this search began could well have been matched by the development which led to the building of the parochial aisle in the church. This was also the peak period for the planning of towns as commercial ventures. Could it be that the de la Zouch family were behind the abandonment of the site of the early village, and the construction of the fortified town, with the little castle, the surrounding ditch and ramparts? In what sense had it been a town? Was it meant to be a commercial foundation

destined to flourish and grow, or was the fortification merely a temporary refuge from the 'Disinherited'?

Some of these questions can be answered confidently from such evidence as we have. Examination of the early Ordnance Survey map, confirmed by inspection on the ground, shows that a very large part of the site within the fortifications was never built on and developed. This is not unusual in planned new towns where the founder's reach exceeded his grasp. On the other hand, there would have been little sense and much foolishness if emergency fortifications were made twice as extensive as necessary.

We have been accustomed to thinking of Swavesey as a village, but it is reckoned as one of the larger Cambridgeshire villages. If we were to consider it as a medieval town, it was clearly no Bury St Edmunds, but it was no failed town either. A glance around the market area shows that it survived as an inland port in some measure until relatively recent times and the coming of the railway.

If we come to consider in what sense the new Swavesey was planned, the extracts in Farrer, which at the outset would have seemed interesting, possibly quaint, can, in the light of what we have seen in the village, now have real historical significance. The de la Zouch interest in Swavesey's commercial development goes back a generation beyond the raiding of the 'Disinherited' from the Isle of Ely. This reinforces the conclusion from the physical lay-out of the town that its fortifications were not intended as something temporary during the Barons' Wars, since the ramparts enclosed large areas that were never developed. But civil war may well have speeded up the development of the town. We now need a full archaeological investigation of the site of the empty tofts and crofts. Were they abandoned for the relative security of the new stockade when the raiders came burning? Are there signs that these peasant houses were burned before they were deserted?

Swavesey as a commercial venture does not seem the failure that some other rather later foundations became. If it failed to fill all the space planned for development this was nothing unusual, and compensating suburban development appears to have started early (if Ryder's Farm really includes an aisled hall) (see page 99).

Much of the evidence noticed so far has pointed towards the later thirteenth century as a time of major

*VCH Cambs. vol. ii, p. 393

change. On the one hand the de la Zouch commercial development would seem to reach its peak with the grant of the eight day Michaelmas Fair. Archaeological evidence in the fabric of the church arrived at as near the same date as archaeological evidence of that kind could, for the addition of the parochial aisle. Such provision was presumably found necessary when sufficient congregation had settled nearby. The 'Disinherited' may have speeded up the shift in population from the old site, thus unintentionally helping towards the realization of the de la Zouch plans. Possibly raids from the Isle of Ely proved such an effective stick that the carrot of a borough charter, crucial in the development of so many other towns in England, was unnecessary for Swavesey.

Borough community and market town. In 1278–79 information was collected of a similar nature to that of the Domesday Book, then more than two centuries old. Unfortunately the returns, now known as the Hundred Rolls, survive only for a belt across the middle of England (see page 139). Fortunately for our purpose, Swavesey is covered, and although one membrane is somewhat damaged the information is almost complete.

The evidence is in the form of answers to questions put to a sworn jury at the Hundred Courts, hence the name. (The Hundred was the local-government division between the county and the village.) The Record Commission printed the rolls in so far as they were then known in 1808 and 1813. Unfortunately they decided to print them in the so-called 'Record Type', a device fashionable at the time to imitate the abbreviations of the medieval scribe.

The Hundred Rolls entry for Swavesey is fascinating and illuminating. We learn that the charters for the market and fair were purchased of Henry III by Alan de la Zouch. In 1278–79 Elena de la Zouch was lady of the manor, and had twenty-four *burgesses* in the 'borough community and market town', which is referred to almost every time a new social class is the subject of inquiry. Swavesey seems quite clearly a market town in the eyes of those taking part in the 1278–79 inquest, but it was not a self-governing borough, and we know of no borough charter throughout its whole history. In so far as it was a borough it was always a seigneurial one – dependent on its landlord.

Swavesey seemed to remain in a halfway state as regards free status. Elena's *villeins* are divided into a group of thirty-one and a group of thirty-two. The groups do *week work* only in alternate years. In the year in which a villein does not work, his cash rent is raised from 8d to 2s. 10d, the difference amounting to $\frac{1}{2}$d per week. It appears that the de la Zouch villeins were not over-burdened with rent; work valued at $\frac{1}{2}$d was usually the lightest any villein had to pay, and he would escape a considerable number of week works in any year when they fell on festival days.

As well as the priory, castle, market town with its docks and its suburbs, medieval Swavesey had its open fields, and agriculture appears to be the main occupation of half the land-holders mentioned in 1278/79 who hold standard peasant units of arable land (here a *virgate* of twenty acres and a half virgate of ten *acres*, but with very valuable common rights in the fens attached to each holding).

Villeins and burgesses. We are enabled by the information given in the Hundred Rolls to make an estimate of population for Swavesey in 1278/79. The total number of holdings is 212. This will probably include some double counting where a man has more than one holding, but this is impossible to allow for since the only clear evidence on the subject is a case of two men sharing one name: we cannot rely on the same name implying the same man.

The figure by which historians multiply medieval numbers of land-holders to produce estimates of total population has recently been increased from $4\frac{1}{2}$ to 5 (see page 138) as more work has been done on family size. Thus Swavesey's population seventeen years after the granting of its charter for a fair must have been near a thousand. Such a size would not place it among the greater medieval towns, but as medieval towns went it was far from insignificant, more like the average.

If we compare the implied size of about 1060 for the population of Swavesey in the 1278/79 Hundred Rolls, it is worth noticing that the first census of the nineteenth century to produce a higher figure was that of 1831, and the population was well down below the thousand by the start of the twentieth century.

There is a note in the entry dealing with the Cheney manor in Long Stanton in the Hundred Rolls which

22. *The line reached by the waters in the 1947 flood, revealed much about the Fens. Here stand revealed the three parts of Swavesey: the Island at Church End, site of the former monastery; the fortified, planned town from Church Bridge to Turnbridge, and the suburb, Boxworth End. Cuts and wharfs in the dock area emerge with unexpected clarity, and the castle mound appears to be defending the wall at the point where higher ground seems to come in as a road.*

throws some light on the Swavesey of the time. The Cheney villeins' carrying services included taking the lord's corn by water to Cambridge or Swavesey. The commercial rise of Swavesey must have made some impact to get incorporated in immemorial custom of another lord's manor so soon. The mention of corn is interesting: as the fair was at Michaelmas it was probably predominantly a corn fair.

Journey's end. The exploration of Swavesey examined a relatively small quantity of evidence, but yet so much came out of it because there were so many different types of evidence to reinforce it.

The quest began in the course of a more general piece of fieldwork, when the clues in the form of earthworks under the trees in the orchard started the hunt for more. Air photographs were used in more than one part of the investigation, but proved particularly useful in seeing more of the abandoned medieval agricultural village.

The archaeology of the standing houses was useful; the archaeology of the church was crucial to our discovering something of the great change in the medieval history of Swavesey. Maps helped, particularly the first edition of the 6-inch Ordnance Survey, and the Enclosure Award Map, which related the changes at opposite ends of the village, and brought all the evidence together so that we saw something at least of the birth of the town and its consequences for the old settlement.

Swavesey is not as yet favoured with much written history, but the few books like the *Victoria County History*, where we were able to find some references to the village, helped both to fill in the story and to relate it to wider local and national history. The printed documents which were consulted, Farrer's *Feudal Cambridgeshire*, the *Domesday Book* and the *Hundred Rolls*, surprised us by their usefulness. Oral tradition helped to save us from some pitfalls, although, as usual, it produced others of its own for us to avoid. Finally, place names, major and minor, added their contribution.

Yet this was far from an attempt to write the history of a village, and what has been done is only a fraction of what remains to be done. Nevertheless, starting with signs of a lost village, we were led to the first discovery of a planned and fortified medieval town in Cambridgeshire.

2 Ealing: the History of a House

'Not all of us live in antique houses. What do you do if someone living in an ordinary house wants to know its history?'

In practice it is obviously much easier to discover something like the complete history of a semi-detached house built between the wars than it is to date a picturesque half-timbered cottage in a quaint old village. With average luck, one can discover the whole story of a modern house fairly quickly, but to explain that story, how and why houses like that were built in that place at that time, soon leads to the history of the site before the house was built on it, and the whole social and economic history of the area. What is less generally realised, something that my students demonstrate for me year after year, is that investigation of a site in a London suburb, or any of the conurbations, is much more likely to produce plentiful and rich sources for the early modern or medieval periods than is the ordinary village. Most English towns need little scratching to discover villages. Most of the history of most English towns is village history.

25 Castlebar Park

We chose 25 Castlebar Park [23] because it is so typical of one of the largest classes of English houses today. It is suburban, semi-detached, a three-bedroomed house, one of thousands of thousands built between the wars, or so we guessed – correctly, as it turned out later. Most of the owners of such houses have never tried to discover their history. We decided as an experiment to see how much we might discover for 25 Castlebar Park in the sort of time an enthusiastic amateur might be able to devote to it in a month.

If the house seemed so typical and recognisable, the road as a whole was very different from many nearby that had been built during the same sort of period. Most estates around this part of Ealing seem to have been developed much as a whole, each street designed as a single scheme showing comparatively few types. The road called Castlebar Park has a much greater variety of patterns in its houses [24], and the types and ages are curiously intermixed. There are a group of large 'villas' at the top of the hill. They stand in their own grounds,

and their size alone proclaims that they come from a time when servants were easily obtainable. Each of these is lavishly decorated with Victorian Gothic woodwork [25].

Then there are twin blocks of almshouses, and we saw no reason to doubt the date on the plaque, 1898, which has since been confirmed. They were built by the Ealing Philanthropic Society. Some of the houses lower down the road appeared older than the one we were investigating. Odd individual houses appeared to be much later in whole or part, and the one plot, most intriguingly, is still not built on [26].

Gates to nowhere. Blocking its head against the road are a pair of large wrought iron gates on cast iron posts [27] that can no longer be opened because the hedgerow has grown through and round them. The footpath alongside this empty plot has cast-iron pillars with an

23. (right) Number 25 Castlebar Park. Houses of similar pattern and date can be found all over the country. We guessed it could not be before the First World War or after the Second.

24. (below) The variety of house types in the one street is rather unusual. In the end we found it could be explained in large part by family relations and connections, or developers, builders and architects, but there is still no satisfactory explanation for the vacant plot.

acanthus leaf decoration dividing the start of the path from the pavement of the road [28]. Originally, to judge from the holes in the posts, the pavement was fenced off completely. At the end of this path and the empty plot, is Castlebar Mews [29], now being completely redeveloped. Again, stabling and accommodation for families where the head of the household gets his living by care and employment of horses comes to us today as from

25. (right) The size of these Victorian Gothic houses fits their date. Servants were needed to run any of them as a family house. The impression is that they were designed and built for people who were comfortably off.

26. (below) This single plot on the opposite side of the road has never been built on. It remains empty and overgrown.

27. (top) The wrought-iron gates, now held firmly closed by the hedge growing through and over them, would have opened wide enough for two carriages to pass through.

28. (centre) The cast-iron posts, whose acanthus leaf decoration suggests a mid-nineteenth century date, bar the path which runs to the former mews to all except pedestrians.

29. (bottom) Castlebar Mews as it was, as late as the 1970s. It goes back to the days when many men worked full time with horses and carriages. At the beginning of this century only Hampstead and Kensington had a higher proportion of houses with servants. Local legend calls this the Royal Mews and tried to associate it with the Duke of Kent, but the map (plate 34) shows that the mews was not built till after 1863 (and anyway was on land that never belonged to the Duke of Kent).

another world. As soon as we start to try to explain any of these small unexpected differences we get engaged in historical research and explanation.

Maps, plans and deeds. We started by looking at all the large-scale Ordnance Survey maps and plans of this area that we could find. The edition of 1893 (surveyed in 1891) [30] showed only the Gothic houses at the top of the street. The edition of 1914 showed development well begun, especially at the lower end of the street, but with plenty of plots left for in-filling later, and the site of the future number 25 was still untouched. It appeared first for us on the edition of 1935 [31]. Even then, the maps had shown piecemeal development, but had not explained this or even given us the history.

We asked the Planning Office at Ealing Borough Council if they had deposited plans which might help us. They were able to produce the original plans for number 25. This gave us the date, 1929, and the name of the builder, W. J. Jennings, and, incidentally, showed considerable variations from the present internal arrangements of the house.

The next source we tried was deeds. The Building Society very obligingly provided the owner with a photo-copy of those they held. These were disappointing, as they went back only to 1969. Land Registration, which applies to a steadily increasing area, is reducing the need for purchasers to preserve bundles of old deeds going back time out of mind (see page 94). The Land Registry Office suggested that we ask the owner's solicitors or the County Record Office, as many solicitors have handed old deeds no longer needed to

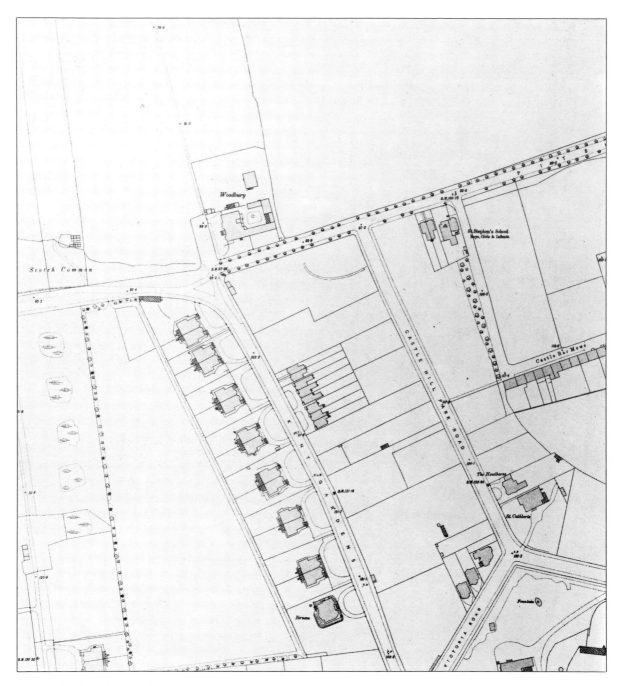

30, 31. *The 1893 edition of the 25″* OS *map shows early development in Castlebar Park, then known as Castle Hill Park Road, and the revised edition of 1914 shows more, but*

the first sign of the development of number 25 (arrowed) appears only in the 1935 edition. So we had a firm bracket for its construction, after 1914 and before 1935. This helped

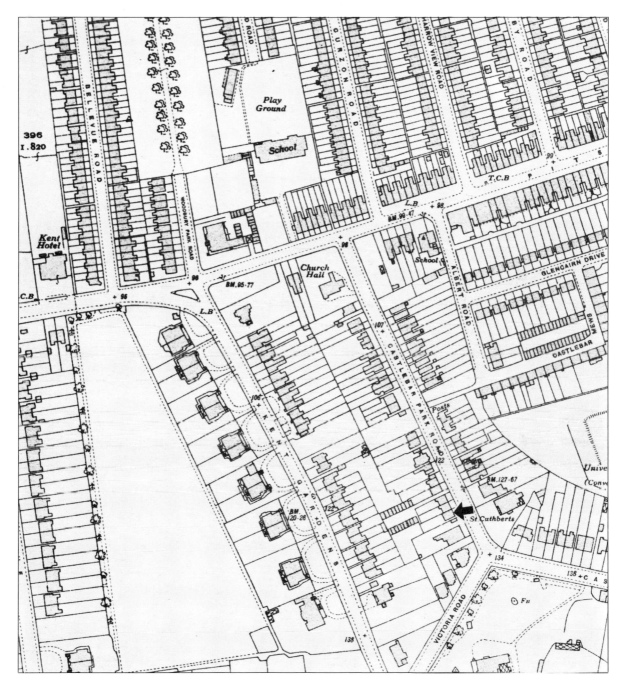

considerably in reducing the quantity of search needed when we
moved into other sources. Interestingly, the footpath but not the
carriageways to the mews were shown in the 1893 edition, and
by 1935 the mews, increased in size, and the vacant plot
appeared. Street names, too, are significant – Kent Gardens,
Victoria and Albert Road.

32. The deeds produced by the solicitor, in spite of most of them being no longer necessary because the land had been registered, supplied a great deal of information about previous owners, mortgages etc. Perhaps the most useful of all was the Abstract of Title, which detailed all the key records in the history of the ownership of the house.

33. (below) The British Land Company played an important part in the development of the site, its function being the buying and selling of land rather than building. This plan of 1881 (a lucky discovery, as most of the British Land Company's archives were destroyed in the Second World War) shows the plot as first sold for development. It was plot 64, and was brought by James Nolder who seems to have split the land held by Henry Gibbon, who appears as a major plot owner. Nolder eventually resold and Gibbon bought it, but for some reason it was not developed for almost fifty years.

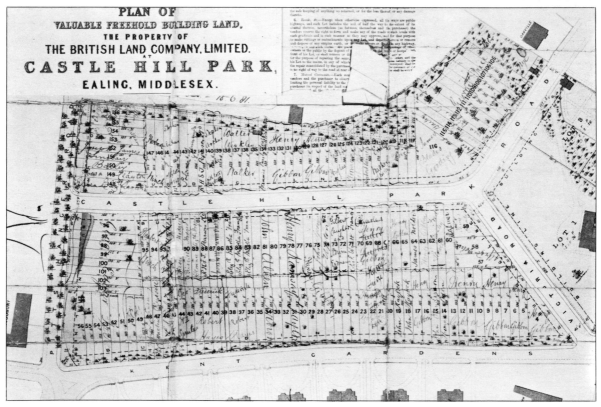

the CRO. Here we had a stroke of luck. The solicitor had a very impressive bundle of old deeds [32]. This provided a list of all the past owners of the house, with its prices at each change, and the details of all the mortgages. The deeds, in fact, took us back beyond the actual building of the house to its first sale for development in 1882.

In that year some 150 plots were mentioned. There was a stipulation which fixed the minimum value of the house to be erected on each plot: numbers 4–56, £500; 57–154, £400; 96–102, £800. The future number 25 was plot number 64, and thus had been selected for the cheapest group. Eventually we found the plan [33] of the whole development, and worked out from the information the lay-out of the different values for the plots.

We went out very early into the highways and by-ways to invite local inhabitants to start us off again from what they knew.

---

34. The OS map of 1863 shows the houses actually built by Henry de Bruno Austin, but no 'Royal Mews' appears. (See also plate 45). The only Royal connection seems to be the Barracks – surviving from the Duke of Kent's time – at a discreet distance, but still in easy reach of the house.

Oral evidence. We were many times offered a story to explain the unused gates and Castlebar Mews, which had stood out remote in the fields before the housing development, and were only today being demolished for redevelopment. These, we were told, were the 'Royal Mews', used for stabling horses by the Duke of Kent, Queen Victoria's father, when he lived in the big house, in whose garden No. 25 Castlebar Park was later built. But, strange to say, there is no sign of the mews on the Ordnance Survey map of 1863 [34], long after the Duke had died, and he had left the area for good by 1817.

But local folklore associates the Royal Family with Ealing in the nineteenth century, 'Kent Gardens' is a justified street name, but 'Sovereign Garden', 'Queen's Walk', 'Princess Drive' and 'Albert Road' make the step from history to fantasy. It is even alleged that some large houses were built in Queen Victoria's reign in Ealing in the hope that the Queen would resume her association (which never existed) with the borough.

The Borough Reference Library. We had very generous help from the librarian in charge of the local collection, and she introduced us to Ealing Museum,

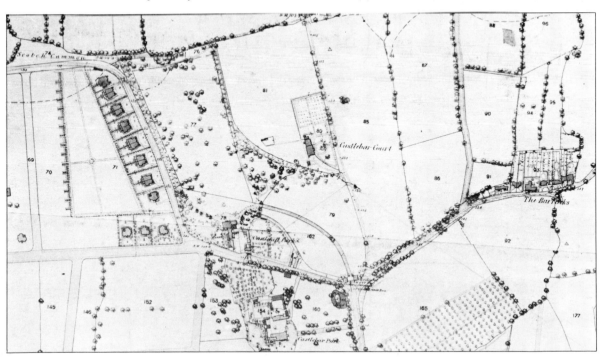

An Historical Map of the Parish of Ealing.

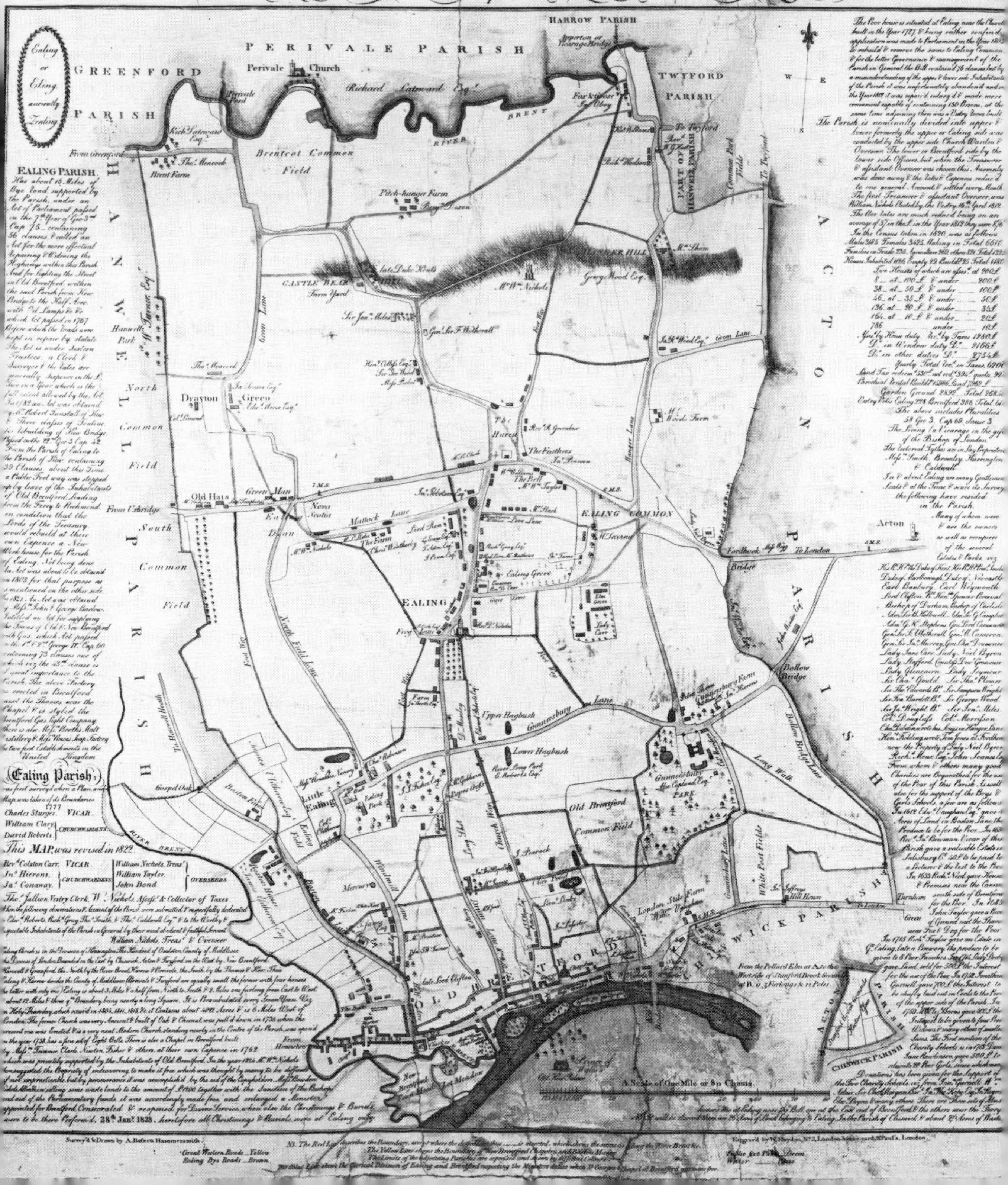

Ealing or Eling anciently Zealing

HARROW PARISH

PERIVALE PARISH

Perivale Church

Richard Latward Esq.

GREENFORD PARISH

TWYFORD PARISH

PART OF HANWELL PARISH

BRENT RIVER

Apperton or Vicarage Bridge

Fox House Inn

Brentcot Common Field

Brent Farm

Pitch-hanger Farm

CASTLE BEAR Farm Yard

HANGER HILL

George Wood Esq.

ACTON PARISH

HANWELL PARISH

Drayton Green

Old Hats

Green Man

Nova Scotia

Mattock Lane

EALING COMMON

EALING

Ealing Grove

Acton

Little Ealing

Ealing Park

Gunnersbury

Upper Hagbush

Lower Hagbush

Gunnersbury Park

Old Brentford Common Field

OLD BRENTFORD

NEW BRENTFORD

CHISWICK PARISH

HAMMERSMITH PARISH

Gospel Oak

Boston Farm

Site of Old Kew Palace

A Scale of One Mile or 80 Chains.

EALING PARISH.

Has about 18 Miles of Bye Road supported by the Parish, under an Act of Parliament passed in the 13 Year of Geo 3 Cap 78.

Ealing Parish.

The first survey taken of this Map was taken by A. Boswderer 1777

Charles Sturges — VICAR
William Clark & — CHURCHWARDENS
David Roberts

This MAP was revised in 1822.

Rev.d Colston Carr — VICAR
Jn.o Herrons — CHURCHWARDENS
Ja.s Conaway

William Nichols, Treas.r
William Taylor — OVERSEERS
John Bond.

The Vestry Clerk, W. Nichols Assist.t & Collector of Taxes

William Nichols, Treas.r & Overseer

Survey'd & Drawn by A. Boswerder Hammersmith

Engraved by W. Haydon, N.o 3, London house yard, St. Paul's, London.

Art and History Society, whose members not only generously shared their knowledge of Ealing with us but also extracted useful material from printed sources.

The printed books on the borough history had little to say about our area except for the connection with the Duke of Kent, and here there is much confusion and muddle. The most useful items in print were the Ealing Museum, Art and History Society's own pamphlets, and an article on 'A Royal Residence in Ealing' in a 1969 issue of *Country Life* by Angus Macnaughton. By this time it had become clear that the development of Castlebar Park was a part of the story of the break-up of the estate which had been held early in the nineteenth century by Queen Victoria's father, Prince Edward, the Duke of Kent.

Particularly useful were the early maps and the papers of the Wetherall family to which the librarian introduced us. As we moved forwards, tracing the history from earlier to later times, the almost complete set of street directories, supplemented by the Rate Books at the Reference Library and the Town Hall, enabled us at last to navigate through an astonishing maze of house names that were sometimes applied to the wrong building, and of family names that seemed designed to start false trails.

The starting point which we chose was not the only possible one. The story could be pursued earlier through the fields. We decided not to follow up the field patterns earlier than the pictures we had found of them in the second half of the eighteenth century. Both the map of the borough in 1822 [35] and the Rocque Map [36] tell something of the same story. Ealing was then deeply rural, with only the occasional farm and a few large country houses surrounded by fields, most of them arable. There were a large number of market gardens.

In the second half of the eighteenth century estates in Ealing seem to have been breaking up and others to have been forming from fragments. Between 1763 and 1770, a cottage and orchard, the heart of the estate with which we were concerned, changed hands seven times, among others to a shoemaker, a grocer and a horse-

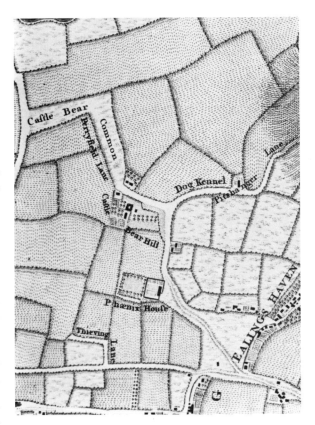

36. The cartographer Rocque has left us maps that take so many London suburbs back to the eighteenth century, when they were still mostly scattered farms set in fields. Sources like this give London's suburbs a privileged access to their past.

dealer. In 1773 it passed to Francis Burdett together with fourteen acres on whch had been an old tenement and farm called Dog Kennel Farm. From him it passed to Henry Beaufoy, who added small portions of other land, and built a mansion on Round Acre.

Henry Beaufoy died in 1795. Mark Beaufoy, his successor, leased the house and grounds to Maria Fitzherbert, the mistress of the Princes of Wales.

Romantic glades for Royalty. Ealing offered special attractions for establishments for royal mistresses. They would be far enough from town for the court to pretend that they did not exist, but on hand at the end of a short coach journey to be ready for the performance of their unofficial duties.

35. (left) This map of the borough, drawn and revised in 1822, was based on a map of 1777 for the boundaries. The supplementary information in the margins shows that the parish had become a favourite place for gentlemen's residences.

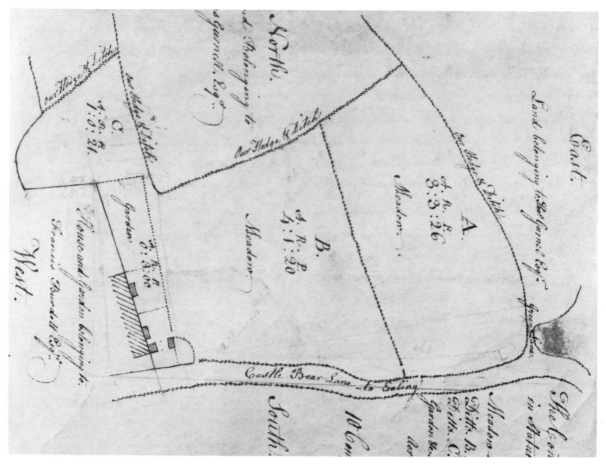

37. *A sketch plan endorsed on a parchment contract from the County Record Office, dated 1790. It reveals Gurnell's land and Burdett's. Plots A, B and C are owned leasehold by the Poor of Isleworth, and caused much confusion when improved by the Duke of Kent.*

In 1801 the lease was transferred to Edward, Duke of Kent. The Duke needed an establishment at which he could live quietly with his French mistress, Madame de St Laurent, away from public gaze, and in spite of his debts he spent an enormous sum, allegedly £100,000, on improvement and embellishment of Beaufoy's mansion [38].

The Duke obviously paid a great deal of attention to improvements in the house and gardens. At St David's Home, which was the house that replaced his, there is a letter signed by the Duke, charmingly asking a neighbour to exchange some small pieces of land 'Between one Gentleman and another', in order to round off his pleasure grounds.

Debts drove him and his mistress to leave the country in 1816 for Brussels, where he could have a little respite from his creditors. The mansion house at Castle Hill, variously called Castle Hill Lodge, Castle Hill House, Castlebar or Castle Bear House, became a white elephant.

When Princess Charlotte died in childbirth, the Duke shared in the new heavy duty on the royal princes to produce a legitimate heir. He married in 1818, and Victoria, the future queen, was born a year later. A few

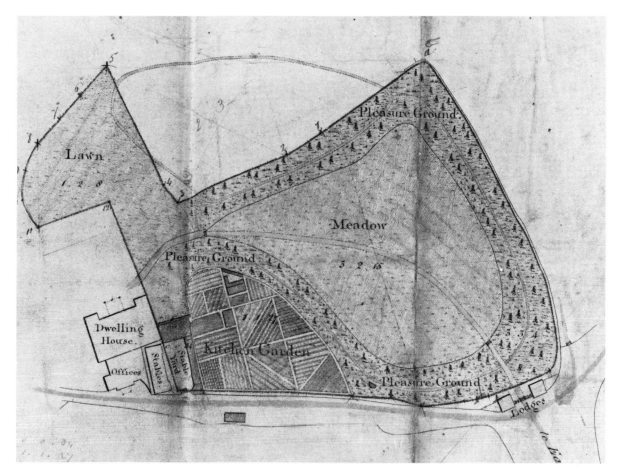

38. By 1813 the land is indeed a pleasure garden. The Duke is reputed to have spent £100,000 on its improvement.

months after this far, far better thing, the Duke died.

After his death his former equerry and companion in arms, General (later Sir) Frederick Augustus Wetherall, as Executor and Trustee and as Godfather to Princess Victoria, became deeply involved in attempts to clear up the estate. The Duke had already tried to sell it after he had gone to Brussels in the hope of covering some of his debts. The Duke could not find a buyer, and in desperation to get rid of both the house and some of his debts, he begged leave to put it up for lottery. The Chancellor of the Exchequer opposed this as a bad precedent, and Parliament refused.

New uses for an old estate. The site of the mansion house and the pleasure grounds now began the slow change to highly desirable building land and a new suburb, but the start was incredibly slow. An auction in 1820 sold off the movables for £14,000, paying the bond creditors 17s 6d in the pound. The house and grounds failed to reach the reserve and were bought in. In 1827, by order in Chancery, where the creditors were pursuing the Duchess of Kent, it was again put up for auction, but again bought in [40]. Three months later Chancery again ordered it under the hammer for demolition and sale of the building materials as well as

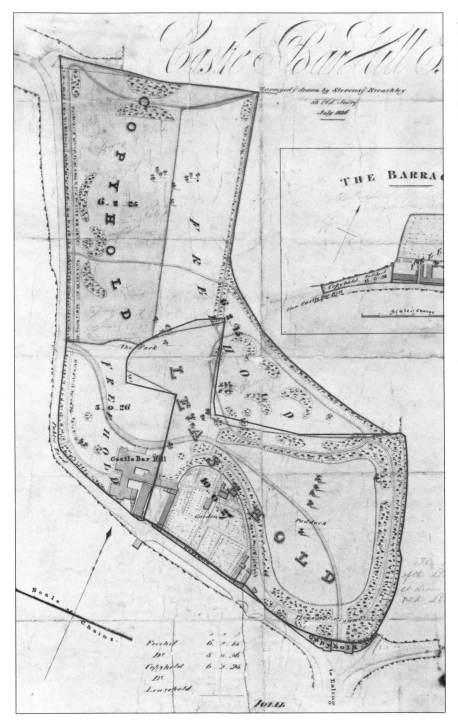

39. The whole estate as it was in 1826. Not all of it was owned Freehold by the Duke of Kent. This was to cause endless confusion. The familiar 'dog' shape superimposed on the whole is revealed as leasehold. 25 Castlebar Park was built in the 'Dog's' nose.

40. (right) The Particulars of Sale of 1827 and 1829 show that the attempt to sell the entire estate in 1827 failed, and that in 1829 the house was being offered as building materials, and the land in two lots. Both sales were on the order of the Court of Chancery in its attempts to satisfy the creditors of the Duchess of Kent.

the site. It appeared to have found a purchaser in a Mr Plaskett, but he took away building materials without producing even a deposit before he became insolvent.

The creditors were still pursuing the Duchess, and General Wetherall circulated a letter to them detailing the misfortunes, urging them to stay their hand since nothing could help them until the estate was sold. Some of the creditors urged him to buy the whole himself to allow settlement to be made. This he did at a fourth auction, but, alas, as his letter to creditors alleges, leasehold land, the property of the Poor of Isleworth, which the late Duke had had from Mrs Fitzherbert, had been clandestinely inserted into the sale, and with its

key position in front of the house it would ruin the site altogether. The particulars for the auction of May 1827 certainly contained full details of the leasehold land belonging to the Poor of Isleworth, and they seem to be absent from the particulars in 1829. In a statement to creditors, General Wetherall asked them to be patient and not to compel him to complete the purchase.

By 1839, when the Tithe map [41] was made, the Wetherall family was in possession of the land. A solicitor's bill gives the date of the completion of the purchase of the Parish Land of Isleworth as 8 July 1839, after ten years of litigation. By this time Wetherall and his son had built up the estate to form a very extensive

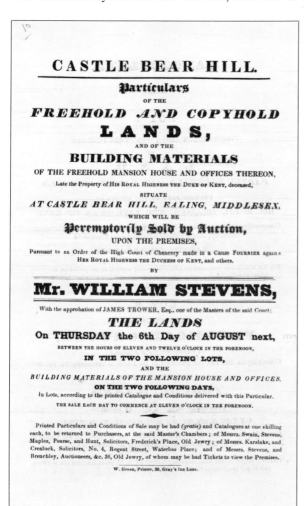

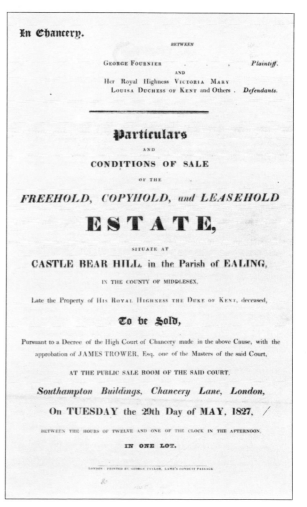

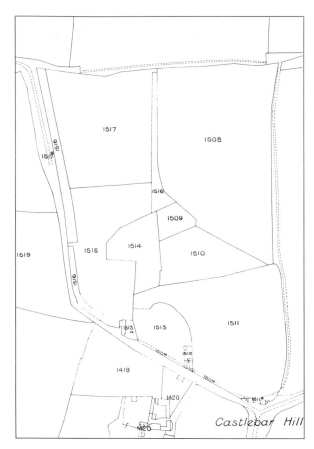

41. The Tithe map of 1838 shows the extent of the Wetherall properties at that time as indicated by the schedule :-

Landowner	Occupier	Field	
Mrs M. Armstrong	*Thomas Meacock*	*1508*	*Part of field*
Weatherall Sir Frederick Augustus	*Weatherall Sir Frederick Augustus*	*1510*	*Two Acres*
		1509	*Paddock*
		1516	*Plantation*
		1517	*7 acres*
		1513a	*Cottage & garden*
		1515	*Meadow*
		1511a	*2 lodges & slip of land*
Wetherall Frederick Augustus	*Wetherall Frederick Augustus*	*1512*	*House, yard & outbuildings*
		1513	*Garden ground*
		1511	*Arable field*
		1514	*Meadow*

42. General (later Sir) Frederick Augustus Wetherall who, as executor of the Duke and trustee of Princess Victoria, bought much of the land in order that the estate could be settled, acquired, together with his son, a very substantial estate in the vicinity. A still visible indication of its boundary is a marker stone with the initials FW *set in a red brick wall at the top end of Queen's Walk.*

unbroken block. His boundary stone with the initials 'FW' is still in the red brick wall at the top end of Queen's Walk [42]. A 'New house' on the site of the Duke of Kent's old house appeared in the Rate Book for the first time in August 1845.

A new kind of suburb. The estate seems to have entered into long, heavy labour in giving birth to a suburb. The kind of life which created a demand for residences for royal mistresses had gone; property speculators were moving in again; but the communications with the City were not yet easy enough to encourage commuters. The critical change came with effective railway connection to the City. The Great Western Railway had linked Ealing to Paddington as early as 1838, but Paddington would hardly do as a terminus for a worker in the City. The opening of the Metropolitan tube line in the 1860s, connecting Paddington and Victoria, especially as the number of trains provided rapidly increased, transformed Ealing into a highly desirable suburb particularly after 1879 when the District Line connected Ealing directly to the City.

The railway found it difficult to keep pace with demand:

Surely it is high time that a firm stand should be made against the growing evil of overcrowding on the District Line. I have been a Season Ticket holder for over 11 years and notwithstanding many complaints I regret to say the nuisance gets worse and worse.

(The Middlesex County Times, 14 December 1896).

43, 44. Ealing District Railway Station in 1903 and the area today. The large advertisements, especially the reduced fares to the City show how the railway company self-consciously and deliberately played its part in equipping Ealing as a home for city commuters. Apart from the prices, little seems to have changed. The buildings are still there, although altered, and the long line of horse-drawn cabs is replaced by modern taxis.

The property advertisements and the reports of sales in this period are very conscious of the importance of the railways, and of Ealing's combination of adequate facilities and a pleasant country atmosphere. One account mentions development land fronting on to Castlebar Road: 'The ever increasing demand for high class villas in this spot' (The Middlesex County Times, 17 August 1895).

Logical as the present development of Ealing, as an attractive residential area in reach of the City, seems, the path by which it arrived there, from its earlier life as the bucolic haunt of royal mistresses, was neither straight nor smooth. Each generation of Wetheralls seemed to saddle the next with its white elephants. In 1846, about the time when Kent House was being built in the grounds of the Duke's mansion, which had been demolished in 1827, we find General George Augustus Wetherall writing from Montreal, asking for his family house at Castle Bar to be sold for £3,500.

If I am forced to lay out £15,000 I will pull the old house down and build something fit for my own residence, there to pass the few years that may be left to me after my return from this country.

Times were changing. In the same letter he says that any goods sent out to him should be sent by the *Great Britain* with Captain Swinburne.*

Ten years later his cousin, Frederick Henry Packenham Wetherall also seems to have encountered some financial difficulties. In 1856, after his father, Frederick Augustus Wetherall, died intestate, the former royal estate was leased to architect Henry de Bruno Austin. As flamboyant in his ideas as in his name, he produced a grand scheme for redevelopment. Part of the plan was completed – the large houses in Kent Gardens and Cleveland Road [45].

From the census of 1871 and the Directories and Rate Books for the period, it appears that Austin still had houses and stables as late as 1874. The path or carriageway with the large gates appears to have run across Castlebar Park to Austin's large houses. He appears to have been the builder of the mews as part of his grandiose scheme. So much for the local legend of the Royal Connection.

*This was the latest thing in ocean travel. Built by Brunel, it was the first large iron ship, and the first liner to be driven by screws.

45. *Detail of an 1860 drawing of the Castlebar Park development as envisaged by Henry de Bruno Austin. The house and pleasure garden in the bottom of the picture was built by General Wetherall's son in 1845 on the site of the Duke of Kent's mansion. The mews also appears, but again there is no driveway into the future Castlebar Park. Only a few of the houses were actually built. (see also plate 34).*

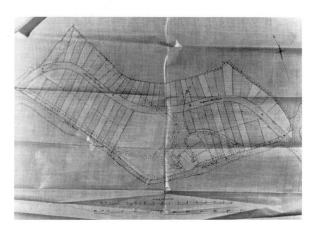

46. *The first 'development' plan by Priest, Pearce and Jones in 1870 revealing the individual plots and the course of the Proposed New Road ie, Castlebar Park. Only the eastern half of the plan was actually implemented. The remainder had to wait until 1881 when the western half was resold.*

The plans of the next development by a syndicate of three, Priest, Jones and Pearce, were more modest [46]. Jones is described as Borough Surveyor, gets credit for the development of Ealing, and combines this with writing the first history of the borough. The land was divided into plots owned by Priest, Jones and Pearce in turn. The plan of their proposed division involved a new road, but not quite on the line where we find Castlebar Park today.

Home again. The plot on which No. 25 was eventually built was bought from the British Land Society in 1881, but was not built on until 1927. In the street is a larger detached house with the date plaque 1912. It was built and lived in by G. A. Mitchell, Architect and Surveyor, whose son, also involved in the building trade, married the daughter of another local builder, W. J. Jennings. Jennings made his living from small scale speculative building, and it was he who finally built the little terrace of three houses including No. 25. The first purchaser was the wife of yet another master builder S. B. Howell, who continued to live in the house after his wife's death until he died in 1969.

And so we are getting back where we started, and

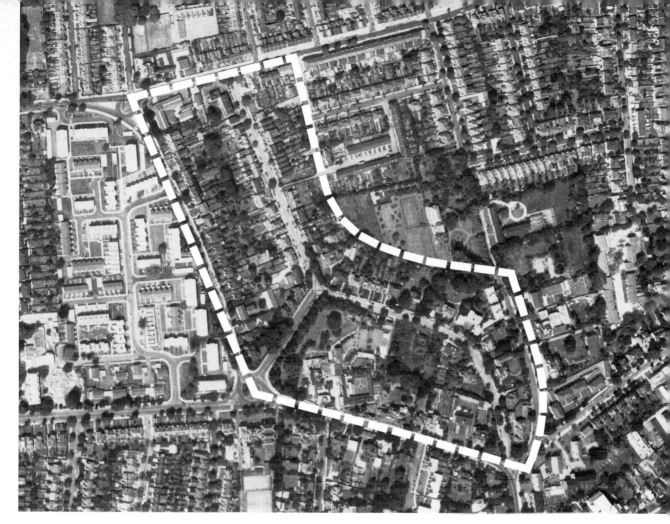

47. *Throughout all the history of the estate from the time when it was in the hands of the Duke of Kent, as these plans and the air photograph testify, the peculiar shape of the Castlebar Park section was recognisable and survives even today.*

know the place for the first time. We have seen the threads of history tying our suburban semi-detached house to the highest English society at the beginning of the nineteenth century, and we can tell a little more why that particular house has come to be built at that particular time in that particular place.

We could have gone much further back in time. The first name we have for the site, Dog Kennel Farm, has taken us very close to the earlier common fields. The Rocque map of London shows the area in which we have been involved as an area of open field and common. The road to the north and west from Ealing Haven was a wide, irregular driftway, which joined and passed across the great dog-leg of Castlebar Common. Careful inspection of the parish map of 1777, as redrawn in 1822, reveals the outline of this common still there, although this belongs presumably to the former date rather than the latter. The only legend on the Rocque map near the site of number 25 Castlebar Park is *Dog Kennel*.

3 Things Invisible to See

Fieldwork. Success in fieldwork is completely dependent on the powers of the human eye. When adventuring out and examining the landscape, the mental pictures formed depend on the eye's capacity to penetrate what it is offered and to make sense of it; however this is normally subject to the limits imposed by an observer's eye-level, not much more than five feet above ground. To look down from a tall building, and even more from an aeroplane, demonstrates something of what we are missing with our normal pedestrian point of view.

From the edge of a ploughed field, for instance, it is frequently possible to see that the soil is not of uniform colour all over, and sometimes the patchiness suggests that there might be some meaningful pattern from a better viewpoint. In the same field seen from above, the colours would appear as the shapes left by the homes or other works of men long dead. So remarkable is the ability of the camera in an aeroplane to bring out these hidden patterns, revealed only in faint discolouration or shade, that it seems almost like an X-ray into the past.

Our eye abstracts and arranges what it sees, but keeps an overwhelming richness of sensation at any moment. Black and white air photographs also abstract from the total landscape, and force us to notice features that we would otherwise have missed. Maps carry the abstraction to the extreme. They are collections of abstractions, invaluable aids to the eye in interpreting what it sees both in fieldwork and the study of air photographs.

Air Photographs

Air photography has the remarkable power of recalling things from the past by means of three very simple phenomena called, somewhat colloquially, 'Shade and shine', 'Soil marks' and 'Crop marks'.

Shade and shine. This operates where the surface of the soil has been disturbed and still shows unevenness. Here the hollows, especially with a low sun at a time of year when the grass is all grazed down, will be exaggerated by shadow, while the edges of banks that catch more than their share of light stand out in bright contrast [48]. Perhaps best of all is 'Shade and shine' under conditions of melting snow.

Soil marks. These work in a very similar simple fashion. As every gardener knows, there is a layer of soil near the surface of the ground which is darker than the soil below it, and there is usually a sharp transition from the one to the other. The top soil is dark because it contains humus, decaying vegetable matter. This releases food for plants, and at the same time is capable of holding more moisture than can the subsoil. Once digging has broken through the boundary between the two layers and brought up some of the subsoil to the surface, the marks of this seem virtually indelible when seen from the air, unless bulldozers or other massive earth-moving machinery obliterate all lesser marks under the scars they produce. Over much of Midland England the old ridge and furrow of its ploughlands were flattened by cross-ploughing with deep-set steam ploughs a hundred years and more ago. Still, as you walk past these fields when they are ploughed again, as you come up to the end of a former ridge now ploughed flat, you catch sight of a lighter, gingerish strip of soil marking the way that some Saxon or medieval ploughman first laid down. The same field will show its stripes even more clearly to an aerial observer, but the cross-ploughing will have produced so many stripes of its own, running across the earlier pattern, that it is difficult to see which *was* the earlier pattern, or to be sure which way the old ridges ran.

Crop marks. It is the same contrast between the humus-laden top-soil and the sterile subsoil which produces 'crop marks' that reveal old works of man hidden beneath the ground. If we imagine an ancient ditch which, when first dug, cut into the subsoil, we can be reasonably confident that the subsoil will be present in the bank. If in the course of centuries the ditch has been left to silt up, even if bank and ditch have subsequently been ploughed flat, conditions will be

48. This remarkable Roman farm-site at Bullock's Haste, Cottenham, Cambridgeshire, was preserved from cultivation for about fourteen centuries by encroachment of the fen. The long narrow field full of earthworks (from the centre to the left of the picture) and the shorter field underneath it (at the left) are very good examples of 'shade and shine'. They are separated by a Roman canal, the Car Dyke, and the sunlight makes the lower bank show white and the opposite one black. The dark field below is bare ploughed and shows soil marks. Rather clearer, but not so clear as the shine and shade, in the field above the hedge running across the centre of the picture, a field with young crops just growing away, shows crop-marks.

excellent for revelations from the air. Where the old ditch was, there will be deeper and darker humic soil; where the bank was, the extra light subsoil. So the ditch will reappear as a strip with sturdier, taller crops, and the vanished bank a poorer, stunted strip alongside.

Buried foundations show up even more sharply, starving the plants immediately above them of nutrient as well as moisture. When the crops start to ripen, or the grass parches in a drought, such buried foundations, or even buried roads, may show up as prominently to the

49, 50. Crop marks produced by drought and parching (facing page) are often much better than any other kind. This is an example from Glenlochar, Kirkcudbright. Drought brought out the plan of the Roman fort astonishingly clearly. Under cultivation (above) it subsequently disappeared almost altogether.

air as any modern feature of the landscape [49]. Perhaps the best time of all is when the barley first begins to change as it ripens, and for a day or two a maximum contrast stands between ripe and green.

Some soils are more photogenic from the air than others, even than some of similar geological type. It is not clear why.

Vertical and oblique air photos. There are two kinds of air photos, one more akin to a map, and the other to the ordinary human vision of the world, where shapes show as solids. The first type, called 'vertical', is taken with the camera pointing vertically down so that the picture is exactly like a map, with all its parts on the same scale and with right angles appearing as right angles. The second type, much used by archaeologists – the 'oblique' – is where the camera is pointed at an angle. This has certain advantages. In the first place the oblique gives an impression of three dimensions, so that a tree looks like a tree, and not just a blot which might even represent a hole in the ground. Obliques are excellent in enabling the local historian to get a very quick recognition of features of his area which were hitherto unknown.

It is possible to try to achieve the virtues of both, and perhaps of more besides, by using stereoscopic spectacles and overlaps. When an aircraft is flying on aerial survey, it will fly approximately straight and level with the camera automatically exposing film at regular intervals. When developed and printed this film produces a strip of overlapping pictures, and with the help of stereoscopic spectacles the ground may be examined in dramatic, three-dimensional form. It is from overlaps that maps are made and corrected nowadays, and it is certainly easier to plot features from air photographs on to maps from stereoscopically viewed verticals than from obliques where the scale varies from front to back.

Vertical air photographs are likely to be available at the local planning office. Many authorities have regular surveys made for them, and for mapping purposes keep prints of village centres and towns at a scale of about 25 inches to the mile. This is an easy size to read even with a vertical. They may also have facilities for viewing overlaps stereoscopically.

The way to become proficient in reading air photos for the purpose of local history is to receive a few minutes instruction, and then to soak oneself in as many as possible. It is practice and experience that makes for proficiency in this as in so many other skills desirable for the local historian.

Maps

Likewise, in order to acquire proficiency at reading maps historically, local historians need to soak themselves in maps too. The more we know from other areas as well as our own, the more significance will be revealed by contrast. The study of maps, fieldwork and the examination of air photographs go hand in hand, with continual reference back and forth. As we move from the landscape to air photographs and on to maps we go deeper in abstraction. The abstraction of the map translates the complexities of the total landscape into something easier to comprehend. The lines on the map, both by their nature and by the shapes that they enclose, offer suggestions or questions about the history of the concrete features that they represent on paper.

Roads, paths and ditches were made by man, and have their own families of bends and curves according to the ways in which past men fulfilled their own particular purposes. Given the original landscape, the changes that have taken place in it represent, by the shapes they have left, the handiwork of people, and it is characteristic of man that the work of his hands often reveals the activity of his mind.

We think of rivers as the work of nature, but as they come down to us today, modified, straightened, embanked and canalised, they are almost as man-made as any ditch, and so they tell us something of man the navigator and man the drainer.

Most of the lines on our maps are in some way boundaries: property, field, parish or county, and in some places can be all of these and more at once. As such they will each have their histories: when and why they were first laid down; how and when they have been modified. They do not carry the whole of our history; sometimes they may confirm what was merely hinted at in the documents; but sometimes they are all we have to recover a little more of the lost past and so substitute history for ignorance. Usually they illustrate Professor Hoskins' dictum: 'Everything is older than it looks.'

Ordnance Survey. In some ways the most useful Ordnance Survey map to the local historian is the latest, since it covers a longer period. It is virtually a summary of all the area's visual history until the date printed on it as the last revision. By contrast, the first edition 1-inch map – and indeed this is its virtue – will omit features which appear only during the hundred and fifty years after it was surveyed. The greatest use of the various os series to the local historian is for comparison over time and the discovery of change. Now that many earlier editions are out of copyright they are becoming more easily available. David & Charles have published reproductions of the revised first edition 1-inch which has had the railways added to the original. Many County Record Offices have photocopies of the first edition 6-inch, and will supply cheap reproductions from them.

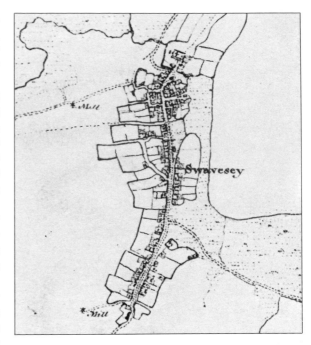

51. These are examples of early Ordnance Survey maps for the same area. Above is a reduced photograph of the Preliminary Drawing of 1811. Such drawings were made on the scale of 2″ to the mile. Many of the fields are notional. The First Edition 1″ (1836 in this area) has hachures to indicate relief and its field shapes and names are much more accurate (centre plate). The later reprint (right plate) has additions, notably the railway, but it also shows, for example, how the path between Church and Manor House in Swavesey in the Preliminary Drawing is replaced by a road, through Middle Fen.

The Surveyors' Preliminary Drawings for the first edition, are available in the Map Room of the British Library and can be reproduced photographically for students, but although they are on a larger scale than the 1-inch, are hardly more helpful.

Preliminary Drawings – a caution. A student of an area where Parliamentary Enclosure took place very late, when first confronted with the preliminary drawing may think he is seeing a whole set of open-field maps which seem not to have been noticed. In fact the fields are notional and the field names sometimes imaginary. It may be possible to squeeze some useful information from them – old roads for instance – but the scale and general imprecision do not help. Where I have found

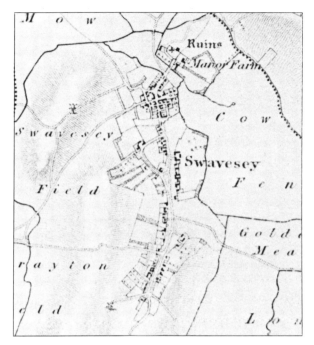 

the Preliminary Drawings particularly useful is in establishing the sites of windmills.

Geological maps. Of special importance to the local historian are the geological maps of the Ordnance Survey. Either the 'Solid and Drift' series or the 'Soil Maps' can hold the keys to many puzzles, particularly in settlement patterns. For instance, it was very difficult to see why the village in which I live, Landbeach, Cambridgeshire, runs along the side of a low ridge when all the nearby villages sit astride such a ridge or a hill-top. A few inches of extra altitude can be decisive in guaranteeing immunity from floods here on the fens' edge. The twenty foot contour runs along the southern half of the village street, but the 'Solid and Drift' geological map shows gravel giving way to gault all along the line. Perhaps this is a classical geographer's site: where rocks change, springs arise and settlement takes place.

Revised maps. Often, if only we can read it, the map contains information we can find nowhere else. Sometimes a guide is needed even to the Ordnance Survey. For example, when a railway line crosses what purports

to be a map surveyed in 1810, some explanation is needed: a revision must have taken place. More recent maps may have a different dating problem: a revision date does not necessarily mean that everything has been revised in the year given. A partial revision may leave in a house that has been demolished by the printed date. Fortunately the local historian is served by two superb guides: *The historian's guide to Ordnance Survey maps* by J. B. Harley and C. W. Phillips, and *Maps for the local historian* by J. B. Harley.

Maps in the field. The smallest scale map which is of much use to the local historian is the 1 inch to 1 mile, in old editions; or its successor, the 1:50,000. It shows the shape of settlements and their relation to one another, and is a useful preliminary to fieldwork. The smallest scale which allows all the field boundaries to be shown is the 2½ inch to 1 mile, or the 1:25,000. Appropriately, the new edition of these is called the 'Pathfinder Series'. But for plotting features in the field or from air photographs, the smallest for practical use is the 6-inch map, the 1:10,560, or its successor, the 1:10,000. All sheets of the first edition 6 inch maps are out of copyright, and photocopies of these make a perfect base

Thomas Cockayne
8 . 0 . 8

Th Freeh.d Allot.t to

Freehold Allotment
Joseph Garner
5 . 0 . 9

Hannah Sutton

High Close

Open Road

Freehold Allot.m to
The Vicar
3 . 3 . 58

Elizabeth Papworth
21 . 18

David Papworth
4 . 3 . 19

Pond

The Vicar

Little Eye Close

Jemima
Tho.s Pryor

Henry Marsh
late Dennis
6 . 2 . 22

Edw.d Wallman

Ann Brapplin

Public
Drain

John Coulson
20 . 0

Richard Williams
6 . 3 . 36

Market Street

Freehold Allotment
Thomas Warner
3 . 3 . 23

Alice Wilderspin
1 . 8

William
Ash
6 . 0

Back Lane

Recreation
Ground
4 . 0 . 0

Freeh.ld Allot.t to Sarah the
Wife of Samuel Thorpe
7 . 0 . 6

Thistle Green

Drain

Public

2nd Freeh. Allot to the
Master, Fellows, & Scholars
of Trinity College
6 . 1 . 33

Trinity College

Master Fe
Scholars

Trinity C.

Recreation Ground

Trinity College

Catlett Lane

Home Close

Public

Private Road

for plotting landscape changes in the nineteenth century forward and back from the date of survey of the particular sheets.*

For settlement patterns of town or village, the 25 inch to 1 mile is essential, and if the historian can get access to the first edition of these, it is worth some effort to consult. For urban history there are available a number of very large scale town plans from about 1843 on, and these are especially helpful since they were intended to help the planning and carrying out of town improvement and drainage. Since 1911 a series of 50-inch maps superseded the older town plans. All these very large-scale maps and plans are of exceptional value to the town historian. They cover the period of the most extensive growth of English suburbs, and it is in suburbs that most of our people live today. The largest-scale plans include not only shapes like bow windows, but street furniture and garden trees. A complete series in many towns will unfold a great deal of the history of the coming and going of the tram.

Tithe and enclosure maps. Most of us can find maps which will supplement the Victorian information given by the early editions of the Ordnance Survey, and, with any luck, others which take us back beyond its first edition. For most parishes there are Tithe Maps and Apportionments from the 1840s. For many there are the Enclosure Award Maps [52], even, perhaps, the First Draft Award Map, which carries us through the great barrier to the open fields. More rare, but pure gold for the historian studying a landscape, are estate maps. These can go back as far as the late sixteenth century, but the searcher will be lucky to find any earlier than the eighteenth century. Large estates, especially institutional owners like Oxford and Cambridge colleges, had quite beautiful maps made of all their lands and then

had these bound up as atlases. The Ordnance Survey was intending to publish the Bursar's Atlas of Queens' College until the plates were destroyed in the blitz, but the two volumes of the Atlas are safe in the Cambridge University Library. Quite the most beautiful set of such estate atlases on which I have ever worked are the four volumes of the Lanhydrock Atlas. These are a seventeenth-century set of land-use maps of all the estates of the Robartes family, coloured with gilded and illuminated cartouches. They are still on display in Lanhydrock House (near Bodmin) now in the hands of the National Trust.

Parliamentary Enclosure will have generated collections of documents, and these may or may not have passed with the maps to the County Record Office. Absence does not mean that they do not exist. During the time that I have worked on field systems, a large number of First Draft Award maps in our County Record Office have been recognised for what they are for the first time, and in the same period it was discovered that in the Diocesan collection of Tithe Maps were displayed some hundreds of open field systems. In the County Record Office for any parish that underwent Parliamentary Enclosure there should be a copy of the Award, the Award Map, and the Act, unless the process was carried out in the parish concerned under one of the General Enclosure Acts. The written Award usually describes from what part of the old fields each awarded plot is taken, and with good air photographs and a great deal of patience it is often possible to reconstruct the general lay-out of the open fields, but the detail is usually more elusive, and needs a First Draft Map, or an earlier estate map.

The supplementary documents are those generated by the actual process of enclosure: notices and minutes of meetings, claims and correspondence concerning them, accounts, rate apportionment and the disbursement of any surplus at the end. In most parishes these secondary documents serve particularly to emphasize the long-drawn-out nature of the process. The date usually given for an enclosure is either the date of the Act or, more commonly, of the Award. The effective day in practice can usually be seen from the Commissioners' papers to be the date of the extinguishing of the old common rights, and this may turn out to be years later than the Act.

*See Ordnance Survey Map Catalogue, 1981–2 (free).

53. *The Car Dyke (or the Old Tilling, as it flows through this part of Landbeach parish) has become deeper as modern machinery is used for cleaning it, narrower at the bottom, and slightly less regular. The commonest width is fifteen feet of ditch with fifteen feet of berm on each side, and when ploughed we may be left with a shallow narrow field about forty-five feet wide. Very rich scatters of Roman British pottery have been found near this point. We suspect some sort of inn, as here the road crossed the canal, and bargees and cavalry might have met.*

54. *Beach Ditch. In 1235 inhabitants of Landbeach and Cottenham were given permission to divide the Common Fen that ran between them with a ditch and a hedge. The course of the ditch was given in detail. The straightness shown in the picture was mentioned in the charter and the ditch still divides the two parishes, although the hedge was cut and burned 2 – 3 years ago.*

Problems of Tithe can get involved with Parliamentary Enclosure. Relatively few groups of farmers had agreed to commute their tithes into cash payments during the eighteenth century, but before its end the combination of Tithe Commutation and Enclosure, by allotment of land to the rector in lieu of tithe, became common. This, of course, meant that the owner of the land so allotted had to meet the obligation on it, as well as enjoy its fruits. The heaviest rectorial financial obligation is the upkeep of the chancel. There was an interesting case at Oakington, Cambridge, in 1953 where the courts held that this duty fell on the owners of the land that had been allotted to Queens' College in lieu of tithe over a century before. The owners were Chivers and Sons Ltd, the most generous supporters of the Baptist Church in the area. The only relief the firm was able to get was for a proportion of the costs to be borne by the Air Ministry, since they had taken part of the land for an airfield. There may even be a utilitarian side to the study of local history. In the same parish I found a piece of charity land that had been lost even though it had been producing rent for centuries.

The Tithe Award Maps and Schedules, and the files that relate to them in the Public Record Office, give a plethora of local information just on the eve of our first fully useful census of 1851. Where later Tithe Apportionment revisions took place from time to time, these are sometimes a series of cross-sections, which give full details of land use, cropping and occupation as well as ownership for their respective years. These go a long way to remedy one of the great defects of enclosure awards, the uncertainty as to occupation and use, as distinct from ownership. This is also a bugbear with the early modern surveys: we very rarely know the relation between the list which is drawn up primarily to check who is responsible for rent payments, and the agricultural reality.

We are led into our study of local farming in the nineteenth century with the descriptions produced for the Board of Agriculture, county by county, under the title *A General View of the Agriculture of the County of ————*. Each county usually has two, the earlier from the 1790s, and the second 1805–17. From the same period, and sometimes from the same hand, come the descriptions by Arthur Young, which contain much material of local interest. From 1839 there is the *Journal of the Royal Agricultural Society*, and this contains some of the best descriptions of local farming methods, particularly in the prize essays which it sponsored. These were all much concerned with the progress of enclosure and the improvements which it brought.

With the help of air photographs we may be able to reconstruct a good deal of the medieval field pattern, especially if, in a village which underwent Parliamentary Enclosure, there survives a First Draft of the Award Map. This will be the map of the old parish as it was, drawn by the Surveyor, with his first attempt to work out the new allocations superimposed upon it. Such maps give a unique 'before and after' picture of the old fields and the new.

Boundaries

Practically every fence or ditch means a boundary of some kind, and boundaries nearly always have some historical significance. Very often difficulties have arisen over the definition of boundaries on the ground, and the resulting disputes have generated quantities of records that have much to tell us of the history of particular landscapes. Tithe disputes can be especially early and informative, and can give us unexpected glimpses of past parish boundaries.

On the whole, boundary lines can be followed clearly enough by a variety of features on the ground – can be followed, that is, in the sense of relating the map and the ground. Unfortunately all too little of our old boundary ways can be walked today by the general public.

Parish boundaries. The boundaries of my own parish, Landbeach in the county of Cambridge, are a good example of how deeply these can be involved in history. The old practice of beating the bounds was a way of storing history in the memory, and it might be worth our while to take an imaginary tour to illustrate the possibilities [55].

Beating the bounds. If we start at Beach Points (the northernmost tip of the parish, where the boundary finishes in the shape of a sharp spike), and follow the boundary line clockwise, we can survey its whole course and arrive back where we started from.

First we have a section of main road running very straight. The map itself explains this with its note 'Roman Road – course of'. This road was constructed as the Roman armies moved north after the invasion by the Emperor Claudius in AD 43 and subsequent years.

All along this section the boundary follows the eastern edge of the road, being further defined by a ditch in its southern half. Thus this section of the road is entirely in the parish of Landbeach, and was finally defined as such in the Middle Ages after a dispute between Landbeach and Denney Abbey.

At Flint House the road swings away from the Roman road but still runs straight. It has picked up the line of the bank of the Roman canal – the Car Dyke [53] – at the point where it was crossed by the Roman road. Saxon settlers would have found that the Roman road and canal bank provided something of a marker which would survive normal winter flooding for dividing the fens, and which would be easily identifiable when the waters went down in the spring.

The next section of the road is again straight after having briefly followed the line of the present A10. This was built as a turnpike road in the 1760s to improve communication between Ely and Cambridge, so that eminent persons, like the bishop, might do the journey in comfort by coach rather than by barge. The inhabitants of Landbeach wanted the Roman road re-opened instead, but they not only suffered the placing of the road where it harmed their interests on their common, they also were subjected to double demands for parish labour to maintain it, when it flooded.*

South of the crossroads the old parish boundary is marked by a ditch. When the turnpike was built on a straighter line to the west of the ditch, the sliver of Landbeach parish thus detached seemed, ripe or not, doomed for building development, being too narrow for much but houses and gardens, and it has slowly acquired houses ever since.

At the south-eastern end of the parish, the boundary runs around a series of rectangular blocks reaching out into the meeting place of Milton and Waterbeach. The outline of their shape is a little too severe and straight for medieval ploughing. Instead they are medieval meadow *strips*, marked afresh each year in the past,

*W. K. Clay, *A history of the parish of Landbeach*, 1861.

when the grown grass was allotted for hay, by carrying a rope, pulling it tight above the grass, and lowering it at the appropriate point to make a straight line. This particular meadow area into which each of the adjoining parishes stretched for a share was known as Harde-mede, Hardmeadow, and was particularly valuable because of its good drainage.

The next section of the boundary, now with Milton Parish, by its irregular steps and curves appears to reflect the position when Milton and Landbeach ploughs, advancing from opposite directions, had reached as far as they could go.

After a short distance following the Roman road, the boundary picks up medieval plough shapes again. The first section west of the Mere Way (Boundary Way, namely, the Roman road) shows a perfect outline of the head and side of a few ridges first laid down by an early medieval, probably Saxon, ploughman from Land-beach. This small section of boundary typifies the way in which so much of the landscape embodies fossil traces of bygone ways of life.

The ploughing was kept apart near the south-west corner of the parish where there was a mere. Plough-men from opposing parishes had begun to bypass it on opposite sides. A complex, untidy shape was left, which was nothing but a nuisance after the mere had been drained. So this corner of the boundary was tidied up in the last century to the shape we know today.

The last section of the parish boundary which we come to examine on today's route is perhaps the most interesting. The whole of the west and north-western boundary with Cottenham is formed by the long, unusually straight Beach Ditch. It is clearly artificial, and yet it is one of the very few ditches in the whole area which will always flow without pumping. It is straight through a very large part of its length, but is clearly not Roman, from the manner in which it takes its one change of direction in a long gentle curve. With Roman canals a change of direction is sharp enough for the siting-point to be obvious where the new direction was set out. Beach Ditch, however, follows the natural drainage.

A dated boundary. Fortunately a copy exists of the Charter of 1235 which authorised the digging of this ditch, and the planting of a hedge alongside it to separate the common rights of Landbeach from those of

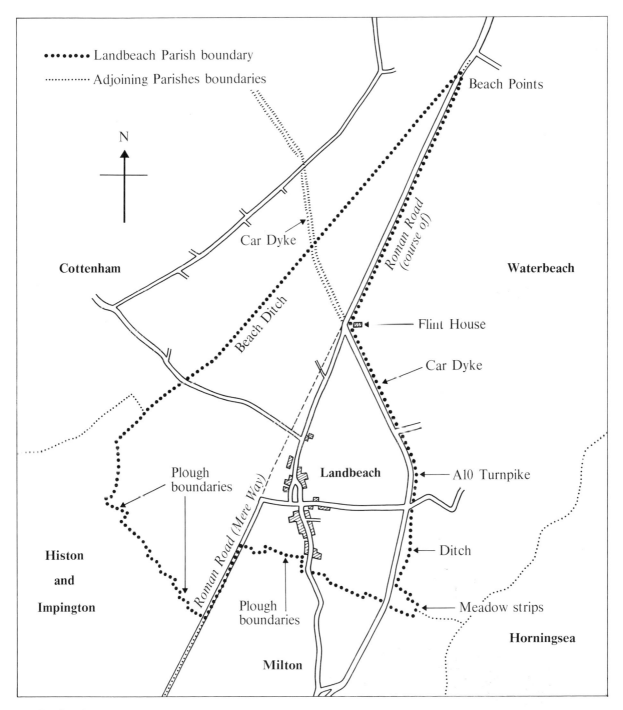

Landbeach Parish boundary

Adjoining Parishes boundaries

N

Cottenham

Waterbeach

Car Dyke

Beach Points

Roman Road (course of)

Beach Ditch

Flint House

Car Dyke

Plough boundaries

Landbeach

A10 Turnpike

Histon and Impington

Roman Road (Mere Way)

Plough boundaries

Ditch

Meadow strips

Milton

Horningsea

55. Landbeach Parish boundaries.

56. (above) The medieval fish pond of the manor of Chamberlains in Landbeach. In wetter times this would not only have had more water, but more fish stored for Lent and Fridays.

57. (left) The Parliamentary Enclosure of Landbeach in 1813 left us a clear profile of a medieval canal and flood defences. Narrow boats in such tiny little ditches carried an enormous volume of trade up until the nineteenth century.

Cottenham in the fen.* Inter-commoning, whereby each had used all of the fen freely, had become unsatisfactory as population had increased, and with it the demand for the rich fen products, grass, turf, fowl and fish. Before the end of the thirteenth century, this pressure had reached the point where the number of beasts that could be pastured on the stubble was such that grazing had to be rationed.

*Wrest Park Chartulary, fol. 248d.

We have been in the habit of thinking that most parish boundaries were laid down in the tenth century. This may well be true. Because it was in that century that the attempt was made to secure enough income to support a priest in each parish from tithes, it was then that boundaries gained enormous importance, the boundary deciding to whom the tithe went. Yet we know that on the other hand there were portions of the fen, for instance, that were still 'extra-parochial' well into the nineteenth century. David Dymond showed long ago how parishes acquired long, thin, straight-sided excrescences, by division of old inter-common between two or more parishes.* What he found was division to give equality, or something like it, in access to an asset like a pond, previously shared in common. What we are witnessing in that long, thin spike which constitutes the north of Landbeach, is something very different. Both Landbeach and Rampton have these straight-sided, wedge-blade shapes stretching out to the fen in the north, towards the Old West River, but not getting there. The parishes on either side, Waterbeach, Cottenham and Willingham, also have wedges, but fat ones butting up in the heart of the fen against the Old West River. These have the lion's share of the wealth of the fen; Landbeach and Rampton not much more than the cub's.

Early villages. There is a good deal of evidence in this part of the country that suggests that a settlement pattern emerged during the Dark Ages, whereby secondary daughter settlements appeared from places where the village flocks had in the past been sent to feed. Landbeach was a fully developed village by the time of the Domesday Book but had until not too long before that date shared the common name 'Beche' with Waterbeach, its undoubted mother. Rampton similarly appears very probably to have lived up to its name on behalf of Willingham, but had become separate with its own field system by the Domesday survey, without escaping from the extensive inter-commoning of sheep over its lands. This remained with it throughout the Middle Ages.

The name 'Westwick' meant 'western dairy-farm', and dairy-farm at that date means sheep. To whom could Westwick be western? Only Cottenham. Like Landbeach and Rampton, Westwick had its own field

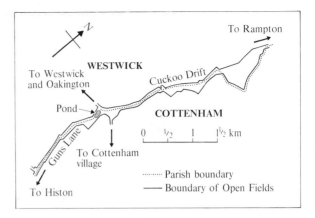

58. *The Boundary between Westwick and Cottenham.*

system by the Domesday survey, but unlike them it did not achieve the status of a separate parish until a few years ago. For practically all of its existence it has been a hamlet in the Parish of Oakington. Westwick could never achieve even a toe-hold in the fen, but there are signs of pressure in that direction.

Westwick's boundary with Cottenham follows the lane, Cuckoo Drift, except for the last two hundred yards or so immediatey south of Cuckoo Bridge. There the boundary moves east of the road, and follows a line that looks again like the end of medieval ridge and furrow [58]. That this is what it becomes only too clear from a tithe dispute of 1317 between the Rector of Cottenham and the Vicar of Oakington. In this it is explained that the Westwick ploughs have at this point moved across the road. What is astonishing is that the position in 1317, after the tithe dispute, remains frozen until Parliamentary Enclosure in 1857, and in fact until the present time.**

Patterns of boundaries. The pre-Enclosure road and boundaries between Westwick and Cottenham are worth examining to study the process of what happened when the ploughs from adjacent parishes met up in the Middle Ages. The trackway, Cuckoo Drift [59], un-impressive as it seems, was not only the *via regia*, the King's Highway, into the Isle of Ely in the Middle Ages;

*D. P. Dymond 'The Suffolk landscape' in *East Anglian studies*, Cambridge: Heffer, 1968. p. 24.
**Cole MSS BL Add MS 5887 fol. 25 f.

*59. Cuckoo Drift. A drift or droveway marking the boundary
between two parishes, Cottenham and Westwick. From being
an irregular space between the edges of two sets of open fields it
became tidied with Parliamentary Enclosure. Tractors and
modern ploughs have contributed to its present state. In the
Middle Ages it formed part of the King's Highway, the Road
to the Isle. It is almost certainly the descendant of prehistoric
trackways into the Isle of Ely.*

it had been the main trackway for thousands of years in prehistoric times. There can be no doubt that it existed long before Westwick ploughs. The question is, 'What kind of an existence did it have?' There should be no attempt to equate a prehistoric track with a neat, modern, parallel-sided road. Cuckoo Drift or Rampton Drift (as it is variously called) would in former times have spread and taken slight diversions to avoid the appalling pot-holes and mud to which it was still subject even a few years ago. The ploughs from either side seem to have had some discretion as to where to stop, but Westwick ploughs went too far at the point where the kink in the brook (if indeed the course of the brook has not been changed there) removed any possibility of discretion and made dispute inevitable. But the most interesting feature of this boundary is the nature of the line left by the meeting of ploughs. Only where the ploughs completely crossed the existing but ill-defined prehistoric trackway, was and is there any sign of the kind of kink or step that we associate with a boundary produced by medieval ploughing. Elsewhere the ploughs have stopped short of each other, leaving between them a very irregular driftway. With the Parliamentary Enclosures of the nineteenth century the modern parallel-sided road was defined, and the kinky, spare areas of driftway joined on to their respective parish boundaries.

Thus a nineteenth-century surveyor could tidy up a boundary, reducing it to a form which would be mistaken for the sinuous line of a forest path. The reason for the similarity can readily be seen. It would not have been possible to steer a straight line through a dense forest. Nor was it possible to choose a straight track while avoiding the already clearly defined edges of the ancient ploughland.

Parish boundaries have something to tell us from their individual shape and also from recurrent patterns. For instance, where a straight road forms the boundary between pair after pair of adjacent parishes, it was presumably there before the parish boundaries were laid down. This a common occurrence and is frequently found along Roman roads.

We also find a road forming a boundary between pair after pair of parishes without the straightness we expect from a Roman road. If it is indeed not Roman, it may turn out to be a prehistoric trackway, and some of these,

as with long stretches of the Icknield Way, for instance, were taken over and paved by the Romans in their own fashion. In others we can sometimes see how the road acquired its modern, relatively narrow, parallel-sided definition, piecemeal as a result of the work of separate Enclosures of adjacent parishes. This can produce odd shifts of the boundary for short distances on to parallel tracks, followed by a resumption of the old line. We are reminded once again of the variability of such prehistoric ways.

Thus far we have mostly been looking for significance in the nature of the line of parish boundaries, but the shape of the space which these boundaries enclose may have even more to tell us about the community around which the parish was defined fairly early in its life. Primary settlement very often takes place by a spring or water source. Thus on the flank of the chalk hills in east Cambridgeshire very long, thin parish shapes are to be found. Each community needed water in this dry area, and so settlement grew up in the geographer's classic pattern at the spring line halfway up the hillside. Each settlement claimed a share in every kind of soil. For their corn they needed ploughland, preferably near their houses and homesteads; uphill from this the soil grew progressively drier. As the population grew, more could come under the plough, but only at the cost of diminishing returns, and near the crest, the thinness of the soil over the chalk made it unlikely that the heathland there could ever be used for anything but rough grazing except temporarily under the harshest pressure of too many mouths to be fed, if the population rose out of control.

Down below, the damper, lusher grass could provide the essential winter cattle feed, hay, without which the plough teams could never be got through the winter and the whole economy would collapse.

Adjoining this meadow, and, in time, extending it, in the part of Cambridgeshire which we are looking at, came the rich fen. When all else failed, the fenman could find the means to survive.

On the fenland proper the pressure of circumstances produced different shapes of parish. The arable was confined to the relatively small islands that stood proud of the black waters that engulfed the fen each winter. Around this came the patches of improved fen, that ages of intensive mowing, or of feeding down by cattle, had turned into lush grassland. Often yielding two crops of hay a year, and rich feeding to produce creamy milk when nearby villages off the fen found their cows dry, the fenland produced the finest cheese in all England, as well as its wealth of fish, eels and wildfowl.

Nearby, on the higher clayland plateaux, parish shapes tended to follow a square or any other shape that would tesselate. The same needs and claims on resources tended to be met by radial development of the fields like a target, with special location for meadow wherever the water allowed it. Here every change from flat plateau had a tendency to vary the parish shape from the square. What we see in the countryside of villages in ancient parish boundaries today is the resultant between the needs and technology of the community that founded the village and the topography of the area.

In the stone, upland country of isolated farms and hamlets, the parish boundary is only rarely the line drawn around the single economic unit. A number of farms or hamlets tend to be collected into one parish, the smaller unit being unable to support a church. Because the process of clearing stone from the surface went hand in hand with the building of field walls, the stone country still shows many of its primitive fields to us today. We can see more of the process of taming the waste on the moors and fringes of the moors and mountains than we can in the milder landscapes of the Midlands and eastern counties. In the harsher topography of the west and north, the stone calls the tune more. But even here the apparent spider's web of field walls is made of more than one simple element.

There are the long, straightish ranch boundaries that run along the spines of the hills, separating the territories on either side of the watershed. These may be joined at wide intervals by subsidiary divisions, part of the same systems of sharing the open grazing of the moor. The massive work involved in building these would have been repaid in saving the losses from escape and pursuit over even wider territory.

4 The Township

The township as distinct from the parish, the built-up area as distinct from the fields, may not be so well displayed on the Enclosure Award maps. It is quite likely to be shown only by its outer boundary, the back fences of house plots against the fields. However, sometimes the Surveyor will have mapped it under the title 'Old Inclosures' as a separate map, and there may be further help from supplementary maps of roads and ditches in with the Award documents. In any case, if there is no separate map of the old enclosures, they are quite likely to be included in the Final Award Map, differentiated from the awarded land by the use of colour or labelling.

The pre-Enclosure village does not, however, take us to the medieval village with certainty. We need to summon up all the sources we can if we are to feel confident in any map we may construct of the medieval village, or of its bigger brother, the medieval town. Every town and every village is unique, yet each unique pattern is composed mostly of elements common to others. We learn to identify and partly, at least, to understand both the common and the unique elements by learning this part of the language of significant form, studying all the examples we can find.

Medieval town features. We might imagine that very little that is medieval would survive in any town, built over for centuries, but some features, such as market places now encroached upon, can be very patent on the Ordnance Survey map, and be seen even more dramatically from the air. Old town walls that have almost completely disappeared often leave their fossil traces in the difference or separateness of the development inside and outside the wall. Many walled cities managed to keep a lane on the inside or outside of the wall clear, with the result, as in modern Norwich, that there is an inner ring road, although now precious little wall. Those towns which had fields around them that went through the process of Parliamentary Enclosure often show a remarkable change of pattern between the areas where development was cramped for centuries, and the large-scale post-Enclosure expansion. Where

the surveyor used existing boundaries and ways, the curve of the street, the awkwardness of some of the plots, the wedge shape of buildings fitted on to medieval *gores* in the corner of a field, are all like the impressions of a fern on a lump of coal, the outlined shape of former life long gone [60]. Any town that ever had any element of planning in its lay-out or revised lay-out seems to reveal the outline at least on the map, and again more remarkably from the air. Most old towns, too, have their archives better preserved than do villages.

Medieval village features. With villages we often have to eke out a little medieval information with a very heavy reliance on visual material. We have to use the patterns we have come to recognise in aerial photographs to interpret, by comparison and contrast, the map and photograph of the subject of study. Most of our information about patterns of medieval villages is derived from the study and excavation of deserted ones, because those not deserted but still lived in are not available for excavation. We can often make a very tentative identification of certain features in an aerial photograph of a deserted medieval village: a wide, sunken high street; enclosures (tofts and crofts) in which houses formerly stood; a larger enclosure, possibly surrounded by a moat, the manor house; other large enclosures, possibly earlier or later manor houses, or even contemporary lesser manor sites; the church in its churchyard; the green or greens, and possibly market place; a *leat*, pond and the platform on which a water-mill stood; and out of the village, up on the hill, a mound shaped like an inverted pudding-basin, the tump on which the windmill stood [61].

Such identifications can only be conjectured until confirmed by excavation or supported by a good deal of circumstantial evidence from documents.

The rental. The kind of documentary evidence that can help in identifying and reconstituting the plan of a medieval town or village is the rental or the tax-list, and the land charter legalising transfer of land. Quite often the medieval rental was drawn up to help a collector in

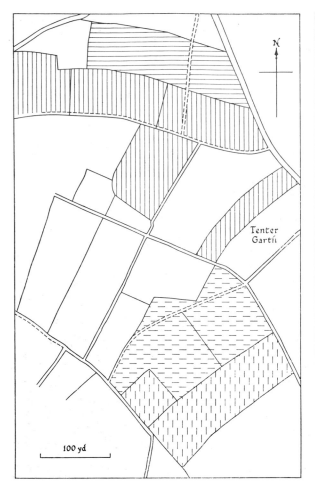

60. *These three illustrations were selected by Professor Beresford when he was demonstrating the pattern of the growth of Leeds. The first plan shows something of what was left of the old open-field patterns and boundaries as late as 1841. The second plan shows how (once enclosure freed the fields for building) hasty development occurred to make room for workers for the new industrial jobs. Many of the new field boundaries were derived from their predecessors, and passed on as the outline of plots bought by developers. The desperate attempts to make maximum use of space produced results like the triangular wedge-shaped block of houses. The air photograph captured this clearly a few years ago.*

that it followed his route around the houses, usually clockwise. There is one for the principal manor of the village in which I live, dated 1459, followed by a

long series of successors. It does not detail the pieces of land which are outside this manor, but identifies the owner and occupier of the land on either side of the manorial holdings described. With patience, comparing this information with the first edition of the Ordnance Survey map in the 25-inch version, it is possible to identify most of the late medieval lay-out of the village with complete certainty.

The terrier. Rentals like this may be as helpful in working out the pattern of the houses in village or town as are terriers for field systems. We are particularly lucky in my own village in that our fifteenth- and sixteenth-century terriers take in not only all the arable

land, whoever held it, but also treat all the built up area as *furlongs* in the adjacent open fields, so that we can complete the identifications on the map.

A few years ago we were continually urging caution on those who wanted, too easily, to identify the built-up areas as shown on Enclosure Award maps as 'the Medieval Village', and that caution is still very necessary. Houses rot and fall down, and may be left or built over. Property boundaries are much more persistent; and although plots are divided or joined up, much of the boundary may survive for a very long time.

The village green. The same rental, which had been specially made and checked, was very remarkable for the information it gave us on the village green. This green had been at the north end of the village (still called 'Green End'), until it was split up at the Parliamentary Enclosure of the nineteenth century. It is still easy to trace, in the long front gardens of the cottages on the west, the wide strip of waste grass and the plots of the cottages on the east whose back fences were its former edge.

We almost take it for granted that a village should have a green, and that this should be one of the aboriginal features. Many must have been medieval creations, although little seems known of the date and process of forming them. Fortunately in Landbeach [62] the green was recent enough when the rental was made

61. *Where medieval houses and buildings were built wholly or partly in stone, their foundations, if deserted, tend to show up much better. At Angam in Yorkshire we can speculate on its plan. The village high street appears to run down the centre of the picture as a hollow way and ends at the pit – once the village pond? The heart of the village would seem to be at the top of the main street where most of the house platforms can still be seen, clustered around what was probably the rectangular churchyard. The lower half needs more detailed fieldwork to understand what it has to tell.*

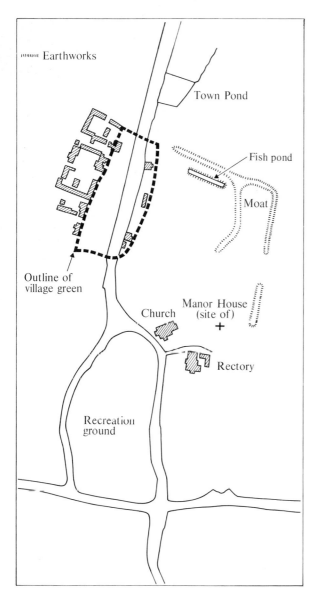

Earthworks

Town Pond

Fish pond

Moat

Outline of
village green

Church

Manor House
(site of)

Rectory

Recreation
ground

62. *Most visitors to present day Landbeach would be tempted to regard the modern recreation ground as the site of the old village green – it is, after all, as close to the centre of the village as possible, is opposite the Parish Church and the Parish Pump can be seen on its boundary. But the real 'green' is some distance away right at the end of the village. Marked on the map is the outline of the former green in Landbeach. It was divided up in 1813 at the Parliamentary Enclosure, and now, apart from the name, survives only as a strip of rough grass verge between the footpath and the roadway, and in the long front gardens of the houses on the west. All the cottages on its eastern side were charity cottages built on 'the Lord's waste', ie, common land. But, in fact, this green had been made by Corpus Christi College, which was lord of the manor, in about 1439 or just before, from a villein's homestead, when no more tenants could be found for it. At the moment it seems unique as a medieval green whose origin can be closely dated. We usually imagine greens going back to the foundation of the village.*

nothing is heard of it, and the new creation drops the title 'College Green' for the simple 'Green'. The new green quite quickly acquired the legal position of the lord's waste as if it had been an aboriginal foundation.

Property boundaries. The first thing that visitors always seem to notice about Cottenham is the extraordinary length of the High Street, with the church at one extreme and the green at the other [63]. Enclosure here was late, and scarcely any development took place outside the envelope around the built up area (as shown by the Surveyor's maps for the Enclosure Commissioners) until after the Second World War.

Studying the map of 'Old Inclosures' and the air photograph suddenly provided the clue to explain the strange shape of the village. The High Street appeared to be superimposed across a group of open-field furlongs both north to the church and south to the green. In between there was a square of irregularly-shaped properties, with the *demesne* blocks of the two principal manors attached. This had all the appearance of a planned expansion of a small nucleated village into the former ploughland of a two field system.

Local folklore provided some help in explaining when and why this change took place. There is a local legend that when the first stone church was to be built in the parish the good inhabitants began to assemble the stones each day at Church Hill, the old and proper site of the previous wooden church. But every night the

for us to be able to date it quite closely. It had been a bond tenement (a villein's holding). When the villein family died out it was inherited by the last holder's godson, who cultivated it for a few turns. He died in 1439, and we are told that after he ceased to cultivate it, it was made into a green. This must have been 1439 or a little earlier, but not before 1429. An earlier green seems to have survived also for at least a century, but thereafter

63. *In this aerial photograph of Cottenham, Cambridgeshire, the line of the High Street, cuts diagonally across what is obviously an older field pattern. Furlongs and selions taken out of the open fields, and unequally divided, in the course of time became peasants' tofts and crofts and are still to be seen in the pattern of the houses bordering on the main street, all of which have very long gardens. A back lane can still be seen at the bottom of the gardens of the houses on the left.*

Devil (or in one local version the 'Aborigines') removed them to the site of the present church. In the end, after much frustrated effort, the Cottenham folk gave the Devil best and built the church where he wanted it, and where it remains to this day. This legend, or a version of it, crops up in several places where there has been a change in site of the parish church. The change of site in Cottenham makes sense of some of the minor place names in the village, Church Field and Church Hill, so far from the church.

In the fifteenth century it was still necessary to unload heavy stones, which were destined for the manor house, in the centre of the village, at the same spot near the church – the Waits – and to employ villeins to get them the rest of the way. The Waits survives as a place name today, and it can be seen in the old Rectory garden as a round drained pond, with a former ditch, now a sunken path, leading towards the cut. This pattern can be seen elsewhere in the Fens: an ancient dock and a large stone church on the first dry, hard ground at the end of a *lode* that would have carried the barges laden with stone.

If these suggestions are pointing us to the correct answer, that the length of the village is the result of the changes made to accommodate the building of a stone church, when did the change take place?

Looking around the walls of the church from the outside, one can spot a good deal of re-used Norman stones [64]. On general grounds the Norman period would be a very likely date for building a first stone church, even if we no longer believe that this was the case practically everywhere. A further piece of evidence which would support the Norman period is the site of the manor house of Harlestons. This was a new manor created in the reign of William the Conqueror to provide a *knight's fee*. The house was built on one of the furlongs taken out of the open fields to the south, apparently to balance those taken away from the field in the north and to unite the village and its new church. This implies that the village green on this furlong was also a creation of the same Norman period.

Thus it appears as if the residual area of the village, the square and the demesne block, represents an earlier pattern, probably Saxon. Perhaps one day we shall have better evidence about this. In the meantime, until we have more to work on, we can use only what we have.

64. *Tell-tale Norman chevrons, no longer part of a decorative pattern, indicate re-use of earlier stonework in the re-building of the Parish Church at Cottenham.*

If the plan of Cottenham seems to have developed in the Norman period and then to have remained with little change until very recent times, we have no means of knowing how much change was going on in the Saxon period. Change is not unusual with Saxon villages. The name itself, and a few potsherds as evidence, is all that most can have to work on. But careful, systematic field-walking in a number of Norfolk parishes by Dr P. Wade-Martins has shown a bewildering shifting of village sites there in Saxon times. Careful recording and plotting of all finds, and reporting to the local archaeologist, are essential if we are ever to know if this pattern applies to other areas. But field-walking, with a little initial guidance from the expert, is one of the ways in which keen amateurs can add original discoveries to our knowledge.

Deserted and shrunken medieval villages. Geographers have for a long time attempted to construct

65. (left) The beautiful town of Burford, Oxon, offers a splendid example of what is probably the commonest type of medieval market town, in the form of a high street of abnormal width on to which the houses butt.

66. (above) Winchelsea on the other hand shows clearly how complete medieval planning on a grid-iron lay-out could be.

general theories of village history from the classification of village plans. By contrast, historians tend to emphasise the unique quality of every individual village's development. But recent explanations tend to see changes in village shape as very much related to general trends in population change. An enormous number of English villages were deserted, mostly in the later Middle Ages, but most of those that survived must have shrunk because we know that their population was so much lower after the Black Death. Most old villages, where development of the last few years has not covered up the evidence, have fields just outside the built-up area where earthworks very like those familiar from deserted village sites show the shrinkage of centuries ago. As practice for discovering these both on air photographs and the ground, one of the best sources and collection is *Medieval England: an aerial survey*[†],

67. Moyses Hall in Bury St Edmunds. The pair of window frames under the clock and the three shallow buttresses proclaim Norman origins. The present frames of the ground floor door and windows are from the fourteenth century. Before these were made, the whole building would have been much stronger to face the mob. Miss Lobel found the town building houses like this on the edge of the market in the twelfth century for letting. Such houses in towns, as in this one with the name Moyses, and the whole group in Lincoln, are often associated with Jewish banking in the days when banking was forbidden to Christians. The first reference to Moyses Hall in the early 19th century refers to it as a Synagogue.

by Beresford and St Joseph. In fact the study of all this book is essential training for any fieldworker.

Thus we have now come to expect changes that are the result of decay as well as of growth in the pattern of medieval English villages, and often see this as the reflection of the degree of population pressure in a relatively stable environment. But even the environment may change from benevolence to hostility through such forces as weather and flooding. The long period of

stability of the built-up pattern of Cottenham does not argue similar stability of population; merely that the process of withdrawing furlongs from the open fields in the Norman period, whether diabolical or not, provided so much building land as to outlast all future needs during the life of the open fields there. Every village is a special subject for investigation, with its own evolution of its own unique pattern.

Town patterns. This is also true of towns, although there seems to be more scope for generalisation here, perhaps because towns are born only in a period in which written records are possible. Professor Beresford divided medieval towns into two classes, Organic and Planned. He showed two distinct types of plan – that based on the market, where all the houses front on to it [65]; and the chequer or grid type, where the whole of the area to be developed is divided into 'quarters', squarish plots, only one of which is likely to be the general market place [66]. Many medieval features of town plans can easily be picked out from maps and plans of air photographs. At Royston the wide street market has disappeared, but from the air two almost parallel streets, slightly wider than their neighbours, outline its medieval extent, the space between having gone down to encroaching buildings. This process of encroachment on market places is exceedingly common and goes back very early in the history of English towns.

When putting up and taking down stalls became too irksome, they tended to stay up, become permanent and get rebuilt in permanent style – or this is the common story. Miss Lobel[†] found another process at work in Bury St Edmunds as early as the twelfth century, when the town built and let out for rent permanent buildings facing onto the market place. One of these survives to this day as Moyses Hall, in all probability a Norman bank [67]. When Moyses Hall was built prior to 1180, it would have been one of the few stone houses in otherwise timber-framed surroundings. With its Jewish name and its strength against rioting mobs, it suggests a bank. As usury was forbidden to Christians, only Jews could legally practise moneylending.

Nearly all medieval town market places turn out to have been much larger than they appear today. At Bury St Edmunds [68] the long triangular space on Angel Hill which is now a car park was created as a market in Saxon

68. Bury St Edmunds show pre- and post-Conquest planning in one town. The founding of the Abbey in the tenth century forced the main road into a diversion around its precincts. The long narrow triangular market place on Angel Hill dates from that time. The Normans enlarged the town by taking out a number of furlongs from the West Field for development, and the shape of these has determined much of the subsequent street-plan until today. A whole rectangle was taken out for a new French market, and its size can be gauged by the failure of some of the encroachments to keep to the lines of the grid.

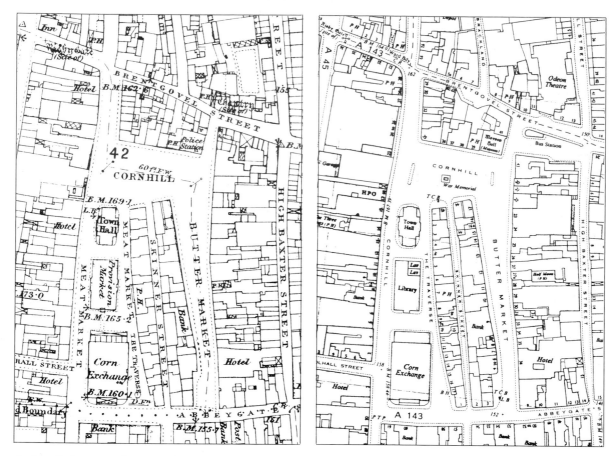

69. *Details from two 25″ OS maps (1886 and 1966) show the area of the Norman Market with its only remaining Norman House – Moyses Hall. The maps reveal a change in attitude towards the Hall in the first edition 25″ 1886 it is marked as a Police Station – in fact it was opened to the public in 1899.*

times when the building of the Abbey forced the diversion of the main road through this space around the precinct. A century or so later, when the Normans replanned the town, taking in former arable land from Bury's West Field, a new rectangular market place was provided. Of this the present market place is only a tiny fragment, and even when we add the area of the Buttermarket, still much less than half. The shape and alignment of the Buttermarket betray encroachment by their contrast with the rest of the town. At the same time, down on Angel Hill, the air photograph reveals

the Athenaeum and buildings to the south of it as encroachment on the late Saxon market too.

Maps are even better than air photographs for spotting parish churches in medieval towns. Norwich once had fifty-two. Norwich also is a good example of how a medieval town can reveal itself from another angle: many of its old street names, such as Rampant Horse Street or Maddermarket, show subsidiary markets and a tendency (as in some other towns also) for the men of particular occupations to live in the same streets. This becomes even more marked if one can get hold of the list of old street names. In Cambridge, for instance, apart from a few names like Peas Hill we see little of this phenomenon, but if we look at the list of old street names that Reaney gives in his *Place names of Cambridgeshire*,[†] specialist markets and particular trades seem to be the dominant types of street name.

The churches and crafts come together in the guilds with their chantries and chapels. The religious clubs of the period, the guilds that we find in villages as well as towns had as their original purposes the mutual protection of members against the ills of this life and the next. They were friendly societies, and pursued their activities through special devotion to an appropriate saint. In towns where the men of particular trades tended to live in one quarter, they would find themselves attending the same parish church and enjoying membership of the same guild. Thus nothing could be more natural than for the guild to become the official organisation which spoke for the men of that trade. In the Middle Ages it was also natural to see no division between religion and everyday life. You needed not only to care for your brother when he was sick, but also to protect him from unfair competition when well, give him a proper funeral in due time, and have masses said for his soul, especially in the first critical years after death when he would need to be supported in his desire to be freed from Purgatory.

Old churches are very likely to have some signs of the chapels of these former guilds and chantries. Many guild records have survived, and have been a favourite type of document for local Record Societies to publish. In medieval towns, after the parish churches, the guildhall is quite likely to be the oldest surviving building, although, as we know, a few Norman houses (probably those of Jewish bankers) survive in some eastern towns from an earlier age. But the recognition of the history, dates and functions of standing structures from their present appearance is a story which will bring us back to towns again.

5 Village and Common

One of the most striking features in air photographs of deserted medieval villages in the Midlands [70] is the clear distinction between the sites of the village nucleus, with the plots and platforms of the buildings along the former streets, and the ridge and furrow of the former fields. The land of the parish lay in zones, sometimes in rough concentric rings like a target, sometimes in blocks one above another on the flank of a hill; or they might compromise between these two patterns to fit in with the local topography. In examining a medieval village it is worth studying these zones from the way in which common rights change from each to its neighbour.

In an air photograph one can usually identify the village streets. Fronting on to them are the enclosures within which the peasants' houses stood. These are usually called 'tofts', and often, immediately behind them is another enclosure called a 'croft'. These the villager could use as he wished, subject to the general proviso that he did not waste the lord's property by neglecting them. The bigger enclosures that often show up around what appear to be manor houses and parsonages were similarly exempt from common rights. Where full common rights might extend in the nucleus of a village, they would be over the green, if there were one, and over the roads and ways.

Behind the croft, alongside the fence which shut the individual villager's yards off from the fields, there often ran a back lane, and surprisingly often it was called simply 'Back Lane'. In most cases it runs parallel to the main street.

Rights that were called common did not mean that they belonged to everyone. They were usually re-stricted to specific houses occupying ancient sites, and were rarely unlimited.

Outside the built-up nucleus of the village would be its ploughland, pasture and meadow, and as most of the time very many villages suffered from shortage of grass, rights were sharply defined.

The medieval ploughland is one of the clearest features of the English countryside. For instance, if you travel through Leicestershire by train you will pass through the ridge and furrow where set after set of medieval village fields are fossilised in grass. Some ridge and furrow can be modern; it can, for instance, be found in South Australia. But the medieval ridges are usually wider than the modern, and frequently curve like a reversed 'S' or a 'C' [71].

In the open-field systems of the Midlands, common rights ran on the stubble of the arable fields after the harvest had been cleared and also on the fallow field that was being rested for that particular year. This usually meant that cropping had to be controlled, as crops could not be grown where beasts had the right to graze; so, if there were three fields, one would have winter-sown crops, the second spring-sown and the third would lie fallow. In the next year, each would move to the new shift in this rotation.

Then the needs for cultivation demanded that oxen for the plough-teams should be kept through the winter, and to do this meadows would be set apart in the dampest ground available. Meadows are often found under the name '*Lammas land*', because, after the grass had been cut and carted, they would be opened as common for pasture on Lammas Day, 1 August. Since these were common half the year and private half the year, they are sometimes called 'half severals', 'several' being the opposite of 'common'. Meadow ground was often allotted when the grass was ready to cut on a system which meant that each man's hay came from different ground each year.

Elsewhere in the parish, often near the boundary, perhaps on heath or higher ground, would be rough pasture where the plough could not go. This was known as 'the lord's waste' in the technical language of the time, but he was limited by law from using it in a way that left insufficient for the villagers. It would be common all the year round, and was one of the most valuable assets. As well as feeding the beasts, it would supply timber for fences and buildings, and often part of it would be put aside for peat or turf as firing. If there was any forest with oak and beech these would provide '*pannage*', acorns and beechnuts being the medieval equivalent of grazing nuts for pigs. Often a village swineherd might look after all the pigs of the villagers,

70. *This is typical of the best photographs of deserted medieval villages. Ridge and furrow of the old open-fields sweep under modern hedges and stop in the middle of a modern grass field on what was once clearly the headland where the ploughs turned. The network of dried-up boundary ditches around enclosures great and small, the sunken streets and lanes, the faint platforms of small buildings and the sharp ones of some of the larger, are all more or less standard features.*

taking them out to the woods in the morning and returning with them in the evening.

Control and regulation. Common rights could not be fixed for all time: some means of control and regulation had to be available. Something as simple as unexpected, bad weather might hold up a major agricultural task, or delay growth beyond the due season. To make changes in face of the unexpected, village meetings and manor courts varied the rules in the Middle Ages. In the modern period commoners' meetings were much more likely to be in control. They would have officers called 'Ordermakers', 'Field jurors', 'Fen reeves' or some such name, who would handle the day-to-day problems. The understanding needed to control the complexities of the system came from working through the year's cycle of operation fifty or sixty times. Old men would *know*. Many lists of village byelaws survive, and where there were particular problems, like those arising from extensive fens, these can be very long. In Cottenham in the county of Cambridge, for instance, there survive two large ledgers, Fen Reeves' Books, containing all the acts and amendments [72], sometimes even recording the voting of this little local parliament.

Every collection of such byelaws is unique and offers the local historian a satisfying subject for study. In those just mentioned for Cottenham, as well as controlling the open field agriculture, the Ordermakers looked after such important affairs as internal roads and drainage. They kept a town boat. By the eighteenth century they supplied their bird-scarer with powder and shot and even paid for exercising the hand-pumped fire-engine. Commoners' organisations, where there was a common field system, tended to acquire functions performed by the Tudor Vestry, and before that by Manor Court in the Middle Ages.

Relics of open fields. In the Midlands the lines of some of the boundaries and roads are fossilised relics of ancient field systems. As well as these, and other physical indicators like the ridge and furrow cited above, there is a surprising amount of precise information on the working and cropping of fields to be found in such manorial documents as survive. These become plentiful in the thirteenth century. As these documents get fewer from the fifteenth century on, surveys and field books, and later, before the end of the seventeenth century, maps of field systems start to appear. Before attempting to work on the documents dealing with one's own local field systems, it is as well to look at the terms and some of the variations between area and area and between village and village which are likely to come up. Fortunately we now have a superb book, C. C. Taylor's *Fields in the English landscape*,[†] which deals with this subject by itself. The reader is recommended to treat my remarks here merely as an introduction to that wider and more detailed study.

We have already seen the medieval curving *ridge* and *furrow* as the clearest outward and visible sign of medieval agriculture. This ridge, the simplest constituent of the open fields, has innumerable local names: ridge, rigg, shott, land, loon, paull, rap, stitch, and most confusing of all, *acre*. This was sometimes differentiated from the measured acre by using the term 'customary acres', or '*acres* as they lay in the field'. But the classic general term in the medieval documents was *selion*. When it came to working awkward corners of land, the term *butt* was used for a truncated selion, and *gore* for one that was triangular, pointed at one end. Only very rarely indeed did a selion approach the measured acre in size; a little over half an acre was more usually the case.

Modern economic historians have used a term in describing these old *field* systems derived from the appearance of the old maps. They refer to them as 'strip maps'. The *strips* that these maps show are the units of tenure, the little groups of ridges side by side forming the unit that each man holds. Too often the books slip into calling selions 'strips', and then the argument becomes incomprehensible. A strip may consist of any number of selions. A group of selions running side by side, parallel to each other, was called a 'furlong' – that is, a 'furrow long'. This would scarcely ever be as much as 220 yards. Local names for the same thing are 'wong', 'piece', 'flatt' and 'couture', and the field-books often use the Latin term, *quarentena*.

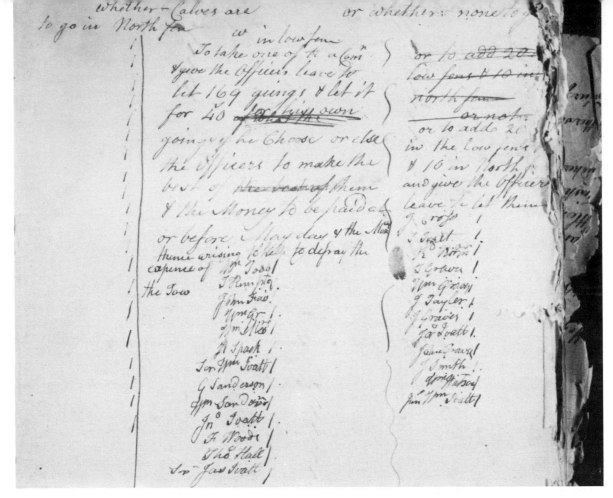

72. *When the Lord's manor courts in Cottenham withdrew from the regulation of agricultural affairs, the Commoners' Meeting and its Ordermakers slipped in. In two great ledgers all the Articles were written and revised.*

Whether calves are to go in
North Fen or in low fenn
To take one of to a Common
and give the officers leave to
let 169 goings and let it
for 40s for his own
goings if he choose or else
the officers to make the
best of them
and the money to be paid at
or before May Day and the money
thence arising to help to defray the
expense of
the Tow. (=the two officers?)

or whether none to go
or to add 20
in the low fens
and 10 in North fen
and give the officers
leave to let them

Voting would appear to have been 13 for and 12 against.

The furlongs themselves were grouped in larger units called 'fields'. An East Anglian alternative name for field is 'precinct', and for furlong, 'stadium'.

In this East Anglian variant the furlong was the unit of rotation. In the more common Midland systems the whole of each great field normally carried winter-sown crops, or spring-sown crops or was fallow. If there were only two great fields, the field under crop could be divided for winter and spring crop to be separated. In the later Middle Ages and early modern period, parishes where there was plenty of manure sometimes reorganised their field systems into four or five great fields, so that each came under bare fallow only once in every four or five years. Sometimes the names of the fields were used for topographic location, and the actual area in the shift used for cropping was rather different.

Whatever field system any village that we care to study used, we can be sure that it was unique. It is here that the general historians must wait on their brothers' local studies before any true general picture can be constructed from the evidence.

All these complex bits and pieces of land were brought together into a practical system by a network of access ways between the fields and the village. To give access to individual selions, paths across their ends called *headlands* or 'havedens' were left to be cultivated after the rest. These were joined up by other *baulks* or paths, which ran into wider, often irregularly shaped droves, drifts or sykes, part ways and part common pasture, that led back to the houses and yards. Baulks often ran along the parish boundaries, and many have names like Mere Way, or Procession Way, from being the route taken at the beating of the bounds which was done annually to prevent encroachment by the ploughs of neighbouring parishes.

These complexities and variations emphasise one thing; every set of fields was special and had ways of working that were also distinctive in many features as well as being similar to its neighbours in others. Local historians seek to discover not simply the local usage in words, but the dialect of local life. If they succeed in reconstituting the lay-out of the fields, they will want to go on and discover where they were peculiar and where common.

Perhaps the most obvious mark of medieval farming in the landscape of today is the pattern of ridge and furrow [73], either as visible earthworks or as the even more widespread soil marks. Of themselves these do not prove the existence of any precise system of fields and cultivation in the Middle Ages: for this we need records of cropping in the village under observation.

Sources for field systems. To get close to the method of cultivation and use of a medieval field system it is essential to find more information than we can obtain from the sight of ridge and furrow in the field, or on an air photograph. With luck we may be able to obtain an old estate map which may indicate the ridges, which are the unit of ploughing, but more likely may simply show the strips (a number of contiguous ridges held by one man), the unit of tenure. Such a map will indicate the furlongs (bundles of ridges lying parallel to each other,

normally comprising more than one strip) and the fields, (groups of contiguous furlongs which may or may not form the unit for the rotation of crops).

The First Draft of the Parliamentary Enclosure Award Map may be used where no estate maps exist, when studying a parish which underwent Parliamentary Enclosure. We may be able to use a Tithe Award Map for the same purpose in a parish which underwent Parliamentary Enclosure very late, after about 1840.

Before maps of fields were ever drawn, it had become part of management practice and local government practice, to make written surveys of field land. These can sometimes, with a great deal of patience and care, be exactly related to the later estate or field maps. It may thus be possible to work out any changes in the extent or lay-out of the fields since the drawing up of the survey. Other names for such surveys are *extents*, *terriers*, field books or *inquisitions*. A local Norfolk name is a '*drag*'. Where none of these survive it may be possible to get some of the information on the extent and even the cropping of the fields from other documents.

Inquisitions post mortem. These are the answers to questions put to sworn juries after the death of any tenant-in-chief (direct tenant) of the king. There are printed calendars, and from the index of places it becomes clear what inquisitions survive for any particular parish. The entry in the calendar gives a brief summary of the contents of each inquisition, and where it says, '*extent*', a summary description of a manor may be expected. These sometimes detail all the land held both by tenants and also 'in demesne' (in the hands of the lord of the manor), with values, field names, the amount of land in each field and the nature of the crop, as well as other property such as houses, mills and dovehouses, sometimes indicating that these were in bad repair and ruinous. The snag about this particular source is that not many have been published, and that leaves a local history team that is to use them dependent on finding someone competent and able to visit the Public Record Office in order to transcribe and translate the original Latin entries.

Account rolls. These documents show something of the working of the field systems. In many manors such rolls were kept from late in the thirteenth century, and

73. *A clear example of the complexities of Ridge and Furrow. Near Padbury, Bucks, the medieval selions, broad and curving, lie down to grass beneath the modern hedges, or end in the middle of a modern field without benefit of fence or hedge. In the original air photograph a circular mill platform can clearly be seen in the small enclosed field on the right.*

where they have survived well, they may tell what was sown and harvested, and how the flocks and herds of the lord of the manor fared year by year. Where these accounts were kept on what was almost a standard pattern, it is usually possible to work out the rotation of crops and the use of different fields. Care is needed because of the habit of many of the scribes of using the word 'field' very loosely. Often they used it quite simply to mean arable as distinct from grassland. Often they

use the name of the furlong when they have a very specific piece of land in mind, but slip in the term 'field' as if by habit. This can lead to very great confusion on the part of the unwary historian, and there have been those who counted every name mentioned as a new field with its place in a system. In this way multiple field systems that never existed have been conjured up.

It is unfortunate from our point of view that the information on cropping grows sparser as we come towards the late Middle Ages and the early modern period. Here disputes about the payment of tithe may provide invaluable evidence.

With the rise of Nonconformity in the seventeenth and eighteenth centuries, opposition to the payment of tithe grew. The method of maintaining a parson in every parish by entitling him to a tenth of the produce in that parish had been set up as long ago as the tenth century. Nonconformity meant systematic opposition to its payment, and parsons in response began to keep a very systematic check, or they would be cheated. In the tables of produce from which they calculated their entitlement to tithe, if they were in a parish with an open field system, they usually worked through a complete cycle of the rotation in order to strike a fair average. Let us take a real example, and see what comes from one simple table:

Waterbeach Parish in the County of Cambridge

ARABLE ACRES			FEN HAY ACRES	
1760 Bannold Field	81	wheat	Highland	375
Denney West Field	64	barley	Lowland	109
Low Grounds	17	oats		
1761 Denney East Field	98	wheat		
Bannold Field	71	barley	Highland	373
	10	peas	Lowland	109
Low Grounds	29	oats		
1762 Denney West Field	44	wheat		
	8	mixed corn	Highland	346
	12½	peas	Lowland	90
Denney East Field	90	barley		
	6	beans		
Low Grounds	30	oats		
1763 Bannold Field	81	wheat		
Denney West Field	60	barley		
	4	peas		
Low Grounds	37½	oats		

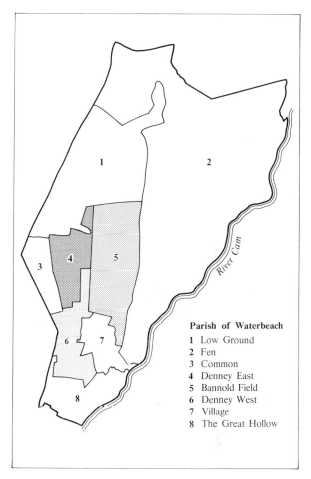

Parish of Waterbeach
1 Low Ground
2 Fen
3 Common
4 Denney East
5 Bannold Field
6 Denney West
7 Village
8 The Great Hollow

74. The sketch map indicates how relatively little of the land in this fenland village could be used for growing corn, and why there was so much hay.

We do not have the hay figures for 1763 in detail, although in total 401 acres were mown that year. But from what is given we can see that Waterbeach had a regular three-field system working [74], with its own peculiar additions. William Cole, the antiquarian parson in the eighteenth century, said, 'Not being a water-rat, I left Waterbeach.' The table shows why.

In the first place we can see the complete rotation: 1763 duplicates 1760, with Bannold as the winter sown field, and all its 81 acres under wheat. In the same years Denney West is the field for spring corn over all its 64 acres (peas, beans and vetches are spring corn as well as oats and barley), Denney East is fallow. One of the particular problems facing Waterbeach farmers was that when the black waters of the fen came up each winter, they did not always stop at the same place, and they did not always subside at quite the same time. The wet lands between the open fields and the river could not be incorporated in the open fields because they could never be winter sown since they were virtually certain to be drowned before winter was over. Only the quickest maturing grain, oats, stood much chance of returning a crop if sown after the waters had subsided. So the picture for 1762 suggest that the winter flood transgressed into the edge of Denney East and Denney West, up against the Low Grounds, and subsided only in time for a quick crop of peas and beans to be snatched from some parts.

The original document gives us values of each crop, and in the case of oats this is usually two for different parts. In 1760 some oats were worth 6s an acre but most only 3s (most of this crop was half-drowned). But it would take too long here to wring all the significance from this brief table.

The evolution of field systems. In the lowlands, especially the Midlands, where the land is not too hostile to the plough, our ancestors improved their field systems, making them more intensive whenever there were too many mouths to feed. Where the soil was not rich enough, or the climate or topography unsuitable for intensive corn-growing, less intensive systems than

75. *This picture is seen from the infield, where, plough ridges can be seen just bursting through the snow at our feet. In the middle distance are old breaks into the outfield, still showing their old ridge and furrow on the lower slopes of the foothills. Against the snow, the dark stone walls outline them like stained glass.*

the three-field arrangements just described survived until quite recent times. These may represent stages through which the systems on richer soils evolved as population began to increase. Direct in apparent line of ascent is the two field system, in which half the land was fallow at any one time.

Behind this system, again possibly a direct ancestor, are systems usually described as infield/outfield [75]. They certainly survived in the more difficult farming regions, and also in districts like the Norfolk Breckland where poor soil made a tiny sub-region where the area around was generally much more fertile. They belong to areas better suited for pasture than for corn-growing. Under these an area near the village or hamlet is cropped every year with the aid of all the farmyard manure to maintain fertility; this is the infield. Outside this is an area of rough grazing, the outfield, from which several portions will have been fenced off at any time to crop with the infield until their fertility falls. Then they will be returned to the outfield as grazing until their turn comes round again.

Both the chalk uplands and the granite moorlands show relics of earlier types of field. Men do not till the thin chalk soils on top of the downs if they can find anything better, and on the granite, once an area has been cleared of moorstone, no one wants to carry it further. Down in the flatter and softer valleys, anyone can clear an old fence. On the moors we find the fields of very different ages superimposed on one another. There one thinks hard before moving a stone hedge.

Primitive fields. The work of clearing boulders from the surface of the land, in order to make fields, was so heavy before the days of the bulldozer that any scheme to lessen the load must have been welcome. Yet there are some patterns of land division, seemingly going right back to the Bronze Age, that have come to light in recent years [76]. These seem to have involved immense effort, but we have not yet understood their purpose. Other early fields with which we have long been familiar seem to have been constructed by men who carefully sought out the way involving least work.

To clear an area of moorland to make a paddock for animals to graze in, using the surface stones cleared to build the walls that would keep the animals in, was an obvious economy of effort. On a perfectly flat surface with an even spread of stone, the maximum return for effort would be given by a circular shape. Again, if the scatter and size distribution of the stones were even, then there would be an optimum size of paddock so that enough stone is carried to make walls that will keep beasts in, but no more.

However, most surfaces met with by pioneers in real life will not be perfectly flat. On a moor most will have marked slopes. Since it is easier to move large boulders downhill rather than uphill, the circle becomes less convenient than the oval, and the oval than the fanshape. But even the slopes are inconstant, and the distribution of moorstone on real hillsides is far from our Platonic ideal that would produce circular paddocks of the perfect sizes.

Additional paddocks could be provided by further clearances outside the first walls to produce loops of wall. Clearance and continual feeding would improve the surface of the pasture inside the paddocks and make management of the animals easier. Further improvements and the building-up of the fertility of the soil in these little fields by the dunging of beasts would prepare them for cultivation and the growing of crops.

The earliest tools for cultivation of this kind seem to have been the hoe and its variants, and we might do better to consider these early plots as gardens rather than fields. In any case, with the hoe as the chief tool of the tiller, any shape of plot would do.

When the plough ousted the hoe, the shapes of the appropriate fields changed to square or broadly rectangular, to allow for the cross-ploughing that was necessary with primitive ploughs. Because medieval ploughs could completely invert the turf, cross-ploughing was no longer necessary, and curving ridge and furrow came in. The curvature is said to be for the purpose of easing the turning with a long team of oxen, and the ridging for surface drainage was achieved by the fixed mouldboard, turning the sod always inwards.

In many parts of the British uplands another type of stone wall, long, continuous, straight along the lower watersheds, but below the most exposed crests, divides inter-common on the all but abandoned moors. These are usually relatively recent modifications of the landscape, products of the enclosure of the waste in the eighteenth and nineteenth centuries. In this process, a very rough rule for dating such walls is that, if other

76. *The stone that makes up the walls, visible on this photograph, represents an enormous physical effort and constant hard labour. Why men have put up with this in an unkind climate from the Bronze Age on is indicated down below by the stream: there are the workings of tin-streamers. The extent of the ridge and furrow on the opposite slope suggests that the efforts of the medieval miner to raise food may have surpassed his efforts in the tin-bearing granite.*

77. Some moorland enclosure has taken place in living memory. Such recent work may give itself away by its mathematical precision. Some of the enclosure in the picture near Jamaica Inn in Cornwall is dated 1917.

things are more equal than is the habit of other things to be, the straighter may be the later. One can see very extreme contrasts between earlier and later, regular and irregular enclosures of waste on Bodmin Moor. On the eastern edge in the late eighteenth century we have a careful survey of existing tumbling walls on abandoned farms, where the subsequent repairs and patching are still visible today. Here the old field patterns were restored. In the heart of the moor, near Jamaica Inn, are sets of unusually precise rectangular fields, enclosing old common land as late as 1917 [77]. Upland farming, perhaps more than any other type of English farming, felt the effects of the two world wars, and for the evidence from the land, we might do well to think of the so-called Revolutionary and Napoleonic wars as the First World War. These long wars and the bitter hunger of the thirteenth century have left their story cut

into the face of the land – 'digging for victory'. A remote moorland farm called Camperdown, with a good deal of its straight stone walls standing, pleads in its shape as well as its name for acknowledgement of the part it once played in helping to feed a beleaguered country.

Improvement by more complete clearance, and the regular feeding of beasts on a new intake, sooner or later bring land to the stage when it can be ploughed and cropped for the first time, possibly to revert to pasture after only a short spell as arable, possibly beginning an infield/outfield. But this process of expanding intakes, as contrasted with the broader division of the moor by ranch boundaries, was not one of simple progression. In times of food shortage more of the waste was tackled for the growing of corn, and air photographs are now showing us the enormous extent of medieval ploughing on the uplands. The characteris-

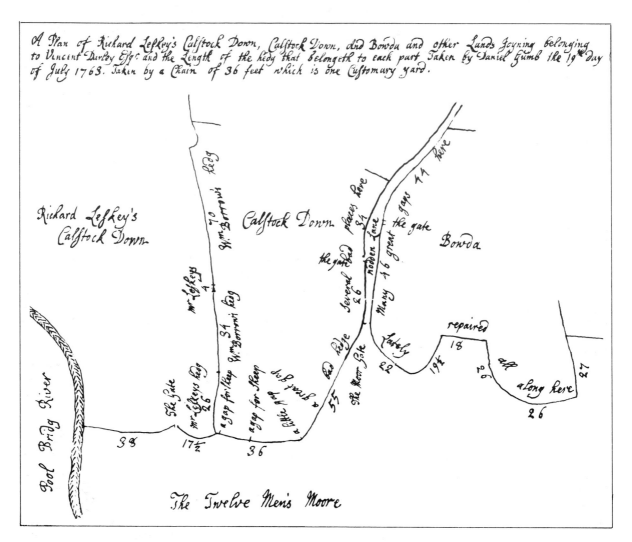

A Plan of Richard Leskey's Calstock Down, Calstock Down, and Bowda and other Lands Joyning belonging to Vincent Durley Esqr: and the Length of the hedy that belongeth to each part Taken by Daniel Gumb the 19th day of July 1763. Taken by a Chain of 36 feet which is one Customary yard.

Richard Leskey's
Calstock Down

Calstock Down

Bowda

Pool Brigg River

The Twelve Men's Moore

tic ridge and furrow appears as high as 900ft above sea level at Fox Tor.

Such adventures could not last too long. The evidence over most of Bodmin Moor is of retreat and abandonment as well as of advance and cultivation. This can be seen in some of the long 'ranch' boundaries, too, where walls have sometimes been built and allowed to fall down; and then either repaired or robbed [78].

Repairs of sections of walls in different styles, and rows of larger stones, 'grounders', with the smaller higher stones from the wall all gone, have their own story to tell. But in moving to the upland and field walls,

we are moving to the study of the growth of field systems, whose fossil traces in parish boundaries are only a small part of the story they have to tell as to how past communities learned to live with nature.

One of the things which the moorland repeatedly brings home to us, which we should never forget, although we may too easily do so in the softer lowlands, is that progress is never simple and linear. Man's advance on to the moor has ebbed and flowed. Hunger for bread and so for land, and visions of the prospector finding untold riches have from time to time driven or drawn men up on to the bleak granite, only for them to fall away later to find respite from the wind and the rain in the shelter of the valley. Sometimes old systems that had been abandoned were restored and modified; sometimes they were ignored; sometimes they were carefully replaced.

The two highest mountains (never, or hardly ever, so called) in Cornwall bear the names of Roughtor and Brown Willy. Among the bracken and the scree on Roughtor's south-eastern slopes is a very long, oval field – or, rather, the remains of the walls and earthworks that formed it. Its long axis lies along the contour. Outside the original long oval itself are two secondary loops of wall. The main oval is outlined with walls built from substantial blocks of moorstone, such as can be found lying on the surface, slowly weathering. These heavy blocks appear to have been cleared from the interior of the oval, and used as foundations for walls, the upper parts of which, built from smaller more portable stones, have been extensively robbed.

Inside the oval are unusually clear signs of ploughing. The plough marks are in the form of narrow ridge and furrow, and, as always on the moor, the ridges run across the contours, up and down the slope. The oval is bisected by a bank along the contour, the place where the ploughs turned, the headland. There is another sizeable headland along the lower wall, where the ploughs turned when they were working the lower half of the field. The depth of these headlands suggest that the ploughing took place over more than a few seasons. There are also a number of vertical divisions, splitting the double row of ridges into bundles – that is, furlongs in the language of the open fields of the Midlands. These internal dividing walls are constructed from less substantial stones than the perimeter oval wall. Either they have been robbed from the top of the first wall, or, more likely, they are boulders ignored in the first clearance for pasture, but too much of a nuisance to be left when ploughing was contemplated. The ridges have been fitted into the big oval with difficulty. Near the end, short ridges and gores (long, thin, triangular slips of land, diminishing to a very tiny, awkward size) show quite clearly that the ploughing was later than the construction of the paddock.

Those rocks which still protrude from the turf of the area formerly cultivated look like outcrops of bed-rock. As elsewhere on the moor, where such stones could not be cleared before the plough went in, the ridge suggests that the plough came up as close as possible to one side of the rock before being lifted, and was then started as close as possible to the far side of the rock. Similar small patches of ridge and furrow up and down rocky hillsides can be seen in the Scottish Highlands and on Skye, and there too this fashion of making the best possible use of land where irremovable rocks hinder the plough's progress is much in evidence.

On Roughtor not all the furlong subdivisions appear to have been ploughed. Some particularly rocky ones at the north end appear to have resisted adequate clearance, or just possibly were parts of a field system which broke in new land periodically, but failed to last long enough for these ultimate breaks to be made.

This arrangement represents a detail in the history of this particular locality: the search which began in the Bronze Age for one of its vital raw materials, tin. Around Roughtor from the west to the south-east, the hut-circles, curiously grouped in compounds, stretch like a small town. Archaeologists have shown us how a deterioration in the climate at the end of the Middle Bronze Age led to the abandonment of the settlement as blanket bog crept down the hillside over the fields, gardens and huts.[*] The huts on the opposite side of the stream from which the tin was washed seem to have been associated with a group of strip-like fields, probably worked by a spade, since they seem too irregular for ploughing. These seem to have been abandoned too with the growth of the blanket bog, but we have no sure knowledge of any ploughing in England as old as these striplike gardens.

Dating the ridge and furrow inside the oval paddock walls is more difficult. In Midland England we would expect ridges as narrow as most of those found on Bodmin Moor to be eighteenth or nineteenth century.

*R. J. Mercer 'The excavation of a Bronze Age hut circle settlement, Stannon Down, St Breward, Cornwall, 1968' in *Cornish Archaeology* 9 (1970).

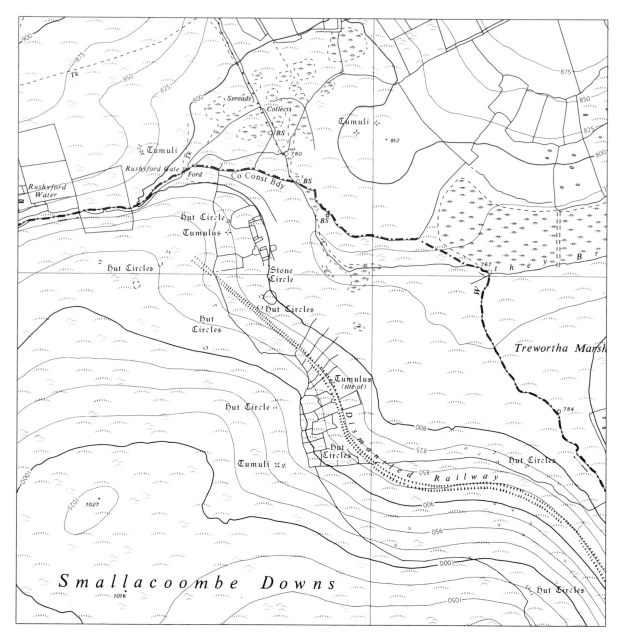

79. Smallacombe. Another bit of testimony to the industrial history of this area appears straight on the map. Tin which first settled men here in the Bronze Age (witness the stone circle) caused medieval men to build a house and clear fields here. Tin-streaming brought men back before the railway navvies worked on the never-to-be finished railway line, and used and modified Iron Age huts for shelter.

But such ridges would be straight. Here, both in the paddock we have described and in other small fields which can be seen in the right light on the lower slopes of the moors, the ridges betray that reversed 'S' curve so characteristic of medieval ploughing.

Here, then, we have a Bronze Age paddock, of considerable size, laboriously cleared to build stout walls to hold in beasts, very probably created as a subsidiary source of wealth by some of our earliest metal-workers, and abandoned as the weather drove them off the moor. Such was the nature of the heavy moorstone that when man came to the area again some thousands of years later, he found his work much lighter by reoccupying ancient sites where so much of the heaviest clearance had been done for him in earlier millennia, and where even much of the heavy building work could readily be put in to shape as usable walls again. The new arrival came to the moor for the same scarce product, tin, as his predecessor. He also looked to the land for food as well as the precious mineral.

With the medieval period we can draw on the findings of the documentary historian to supplement what we have taken from the archaeologist and his sources. Dr John Hatcher, studying the Duchy of Cornwall, showed how licences to assart (break in the waste for cultivation), regularly granted in previous years, ceased suddenly and dramatically in 1348. The visitation of the Black Death seemed to have ended the period of medieval colonisation of the moor. The miner returned to seek for tin, but he seems to have been less interested in the struggle to wring corn from the harsh soil at such bleak heights. In the White Book of Cornwall for 1360 we hear of Abraham the Tinner who held a series of workings that his grandfather had had in the valley of the River Fowey. At the head of the list is Smallacombe, still identifiable, and excavated in the nineteenth century [79]. From the excavator's report, when we discount some of the more romantic ideas of the time, we can get a glimpse of the living conditions of the late medieval miners, and go a little way, perhaps, to distinguish between the remains left by men from such different periods after the same prize.

Smallacombe as we know it today is very difficult to decipher, partly because of the complexity of the mixture of such different ages, from its early Bronze Age stone circles to the shelters of the Victorian navvies who constructed the railway line; but even more because of the afforestation with out-of-place, destructive conifers. But at the south-eastern edge of the moor, on Langstone Down, the evening sun reveals at least three quite different sets of boundaries superimposed. Here there is every suggestion of complete adandonment between each type of settlement.

6 Vernacular Houses and their Successors

One of the most attractive aspects of local history is finding something of the story of your own house. If the house in which you live seems less than a hundred years old – and this is often very obvious – start from the first edition of the 25-inch Ordnance Survey map. This is such an excellent help that it is worth some effort to get access to a photocopy at least. If this is not possible, the same edition of the 6-inch map may just enable you to identify your own house, when it has appeared. If you live in a town, you may be able to follow up by consulting any town plans that are in your County Record Office. In the country, you will have to manage with the later editions of the maps. This may show that your house first appeared as part of a major development, and you may even arrive at a bracket of dates – for example, not on a first edition surveyed in 1878 in this area, but on the first revision of 1896.

Deposited Plans. Large developments and improvements from the 1870s on should have produced 'Deposited Plans' which, if they survive, are almost certainly now in the keeping of the County Record Office. You may be able to discover a set of these for the development of which the building of your house was part. It is possible also that the County Record Office, or the Local Collection in your County Library, have collected particulars and plans of sales. If you have a close enough date to make a search of advertisements in the local newspaper practical, you may find your house when it was first offered for sale.

Deeds and solicitors. Hunting for the history of a single house can be very difficult, although you can be lucky. Rowland Parker, in his delightful book, *Cottage on the green*, tells how his labours earned a little luck at vital stages. Changes in the law, and land registration in some areas, have decreased the chance of finding the kinds of old title deeds to a house that will help you discover its history. But sometimes, even now, the lawyer will have kept a separate bundle of the old deeds which are no longer necessary, and these are the useful ones for the historian. 'Abstracts of Title' may summarise the history of the ownership of your house for part or all of its time.

Land Registration. In areas where compulsory land registration has not yet been introduced, the deeds of any house are likely to be with the owner's solicitor, the Building Society, or other mortgage holder. Where land has been registered with HM Land Registry most deeds will have been returned to the solicitor who handled the first registration. They may have been passed on as separate bundles of 'Old Deeds' to the solicitors of later purchasers. Deeds lodged in the registry after the first registration are usually retained there.

The area over which registration is compulsory is gradually being extended. Where it operates, property can be conveyed without the kind of major historical research that the old type of search of title involved. But as the legal burden of conveyancing is so reduced, the local historian finds his task made more difficult as the evidence to be found in old deeds dwindles.

Rate Books. Perhaps the best way – perhaps the only way – to work out the history of a very old house is to reconstitute all the houses of the parish as far as possible. It may be possible to trace ownership for generations back from 1831, when Land Tax was abolished, by the use of the Land Tax Assessments in the records of the Quarter Sessions, now probably in the County Record Office. It may be possible to follow a similar procedure forward in time from the same starting date from Rate Books, if sufficient survive. Some old rate lists appear in account books, usually Churchwardens' in the Parish Chest, and may substantially overlap the last Land Tax Assessments.

In my own village we have 'A Rate for the Clerk's Wages' from the seventeenth century, but have to rely on lists in field-books and elsewhere to bridge some of the gaps thereafter. The rate list divided the village into Land End and Green End, and the east and west side of the road in each End, and indicated where the list started from, north or south, in each section. This gave a close indentification of where each family was living.

80, 81. Blisland's old manor house, facing one of the rare, but very lovely, village greens in Cornwall, is much older than it appears. As we pass by its end, and see the cross-wing behind, we see the raised entrance to a roundheaded doorway with chevron decoration over. All these are Norman features and Blisland was a royal manor at that time.

Even if other lists can be linked with a key like our 'Rate for the Clerk's Wages', it is always necessary to check the archaeology of the house to see if it is possible that the present house was standing at the date of our list. It is easy to think we are following the history of a house through rate and tax lists, when we are in fact following a site which may have had several houses built and rebuilt on it. This is especially likely where there are gaps in the lists, and could also be the situation with Rate Books. More than any other important document these seem to be lying around unrecorded in private hands, but since there were so many, they will often yield a good deal of the outline of the descent of the properties in the parish.

Domesday. The best set of instructions in print on hunting the documentary history of houses is to be found in David Iredale's *Discovering your old house*,[†] published by Shire Publications. It should no longer be necessary to report of the search what a small girl in our family used to report of her games of Patience, 'It came out with only two little cheats'. When you see that a particular house was 'mentioned in Domesday Book', disbelieve it on principle. Domesday Book shows 'manors, manors everywhere', and most of the estates so described would have had principal houses on them in 1086, when the Domesday Survey was made. A manor house standing today as a lineal descendant of a Domesday manor has scarcely a chance of containing any fragments of the Norman house (if there was one). It can happen, as at Blisland [81] in Cornwall, but the modern house may not even be on the old site. If you think it is, start looking for pottery fragments in the garden; they could be interesting.

Dating a house. One apparent gift for dating some houses is a date-stone over the door or in some other prominent place. Where I last lived I had '1834' carved in the brick by one door of my garage, and '1967' over the main doors to it. Some old stables had been converted by putting in double doors, and the builder had decided to date his work. The date 1834 was probably that of the stables; the house was older still. A favourite time for putting dates on houses is not so often when they are being built as when they are renovated.

Most of the history of old houses, especially where the less wealthy lived, has to be recovered archaeologically from houses that are being lived in while they are being investigated. This means that they cannot be dated very closely, but rather can be recognised as belonging to particular stylistic phases. Careful analysis of features and plans of houses that are datable has provided a guide for this looser type of dating by comparison of types.

In the process, something like a history of the English vernacular house has been built up, which not only helps the rather technical process of assigning probable dates, but which, through a better understanding of the use of the houses through their contents and furnishings, sheds light on the way of life of the people that we are discovering locally.

Houses of the Middle Ages. Ordinary people's houses from the Middle Ages have all gone, and what we know of them comes from excavation. At that time the evidence suggests two main kinds of houses, halls of one storey, open to the rafters, clearly descended from the halls of sagas, and small, one- or two-roomed houses

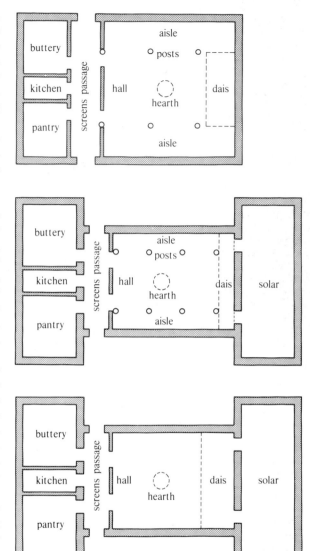

82. Three variations on the larger houses of the medieval village. They would correspond to very small modern farmhouses. In the thirteenth century the hall of a house of any size at all would have had aisles. Already the three main functions of a house were becoming clear, the Hall for general living, eating and drinking; the service end for storing and preparing food and drink, the pantry, buttery and kitchen (the kitchen might be detached across the yard) and the solar, private rooms including bed-rooms for the master and mistress of the house and family. In the fourteenth century the aisles begin to disappear.

83. Boothby Pagnell manor house – Lincolnshire. The type of house we saw in Moyses Hall (67) was very similar to the kind of manor house found in the stone country at the same time, the first floor hall with, below it, an undercroft for storage. Entrance could only be made at first floor level by an outside stair. These are very early, and in the thirteenth century it was common to replace them with aisled halls.

of very poor quality, again open to the rafters with an open hearth on the floor. These are usually depicted as windowless, often without doors.

But the documents may have something to tell which archaeology might not be able to discover. When aged villeins retired in the thirteenth and fourteenth centuries they often recorded the arrangements between the two generations in the court rolls. The name for the part of the house that would go to the old folk, *receptaculum*, was supposed to be one third of the whole, but it usually consisted of two rooms – a bower and chamber, most often. Where accommodation was not of this standard, the arrangement might make provision for the extension or addition of a room. One gets the impression of a chain of buildings or rooms of some kind. The alteration or rebuilding which the archaeologists have discovered to take place so frequently in the peasants' houses may in part, at least, be not so much an expression of poverty as massive do-it-yourself, to respond to changing family needs. So too is the lack of windows and doors in doubt: in my own village the peasants robbed the houses, left empty by the Black Death, of doors, window shutters and various other timber.*

Hall houses. Although, as far as we know, the peasants' houses of this period have all gone, some of the larger halls survive. The earliest timber ones seem all to have been aisled [82], and to have been most common and at their finest in the South-East, in so many ways the pace-setter in the fashion of vernacular housing. (By

*J. R. Ravensdale *Liable to floods*, p. 160.

84. In this Manor House at Little Chesterford, Essex, we have almost a complete history of the English medieval manor house in one building. The striking thing in the external appearance of this house is the long 'cat slide' roof (see plate 6) over the middle range. This usually suggests an aisled hall. But as with all old houses this one has a history rather than a date. The cross wing on the right has been converted from being the whole of the original thirteenth manor house built of stone with a first floor hall. When fashion added to this a timber-framed aisled hall, it remained as a solar wing. The other wing was added at some stage, and the hall was given a ceiling and floor above.

85. The interior of the original hall of the first stone house shows much care taken in embellishing various features. The masonry in the corner at the left may well be the original first floor entrance.

'*vernacular*' we mean of traditional materials and style, local in time and place, and poorer than the houses of the local aristocracy.) The reason for the pre-eminence of the South-East of the country in the quality of its vernacular housing is usually attributed to economic advance natural to the bridge between London and the Continent, but Kent was notably the freest part of England, and this may have had much to do with yeomen and proto-yeomen going in for display.*

The timber houses that survive from this period would mostly have been manor houses.

In houses of stone construction we can get back perhaps a little earlier. Boothby Pagnell manor house in Lincolnshire [83] is a fine example of a stone type that was important in the Norman period, a first floor hall with a first-floor entrance over a vaulted undercroft for storage purposes. The fire-proof, defensible quality of these led to Jewish bankers and merchants adopting them in the towns even where there was no good local building stone. Numbers survive today in Lincoln, Stamford, Bury St Edmunds and Norwich – and Cambridge has one solitary survivor out of at least seven.

By the thirteenth century these upper storey halls were disappearing as aisled halls replaced them. The

*E. Mercer, *English vernacular houses*, HMSO for RCHM, 1975.

86. This is a splendid example of an aisled hall house of the fourteenth century at St Osyth, Essex. The cross wings are later, but the long 'cat slide' roof, which comes down almost to head height, indicates the presence of aisles.

87. This fifteenth-century house at Guilden Morden, Cambridgeshire, had a hall open to the rafters but no aisles. The different levels of ridge and eaves in hall and cross wings suggest that the hall was one-storey, and the cross wings were two-storeys when originally built.

88. When this fourteenth-century house at Barrington, Cambridgeshire, was modernised and an upper floor inserted in the seventeenth century, the aisle in the middle range was removed to provide light for the upstairs rooms. This leaves a tell-tale trace in the length that the two cross wings project (c.f. plate 86).

89. *The English medieval house: Aisled hall – fourteenth century; Aisleless hall – fifteenth to sixteenth century; Two storeyed pseudo hall – sixteenth to seventeenth century;*

'Wealden' House – Hall House with Hall and Crosswings under a single ridge – late fourteenth to early sixteenth century.

early vernacular aisled halls are a clear example of the process by which men of local importance aped the aristocracy, and so led a downwards diffusion of architectural fashion.

The open halls, both aisled and unaisled, for all that they could show of a whole range of variation, tended always to have provision for three types of function. The upper end of the hall and beyond was for the family. Often the family dined at high table on a dais, and the family's private rooms were in a block reached from the hall through a door behind the high table. At the other end, the food was kept and prepared in a service block and served to the hall through pairs of doors through the screens passage. The end blocks were often two storeyed from the start, but all the possible varieties appear from two two-storeyed end blocks to one single-storeyed end block.

The only rival in the opulence of its vernacular to the South-East in the later Middle Ages is the West Riding of Yorkshire, and when one thinks of the development of the cloth industry that produced Lavenham, and realises that it was also migrating to Yorkshire, it is possible that the economic argument for the South-East's architectural predominance at that period may be reinforced. The West Riding houses which survive from this period were often part stone from the start, and by now are mostly stone-clad.

The discovery of a Jew's House from the Norman period or of an aisled hall from a little later is a great feather in any local historian's cap. In large parts of the country it is the existence of aisles which is the most likely indicator of our oldest houses still standing in any significant numbers.

We must never, even when performing routine tasks in pursuit of local history, forget that we can be lucky. It is sometimes possible to stumble on references to a

house being 'new builded' in a datable document. For instance, photographs survive of a fine example of a Wealden-type house that was destroyed by fire in the village of Willingham [90]. It looks in its photographs as if it were still an open-hall house. It had been described in 1487 as 'new builded'. So this style of house, associated with Kent and Sussex, the leaders of medieval housing fashion, was to be found also in a remote fenland village by the end of the Middle Ages.

Peasant houses. At the same time as the aisled halls and the earlier open halls were being built, the tradition of the lesser buildings which the archaeologists have indicated in poor, one- or two-roomed peasant huts continued. These later medieval peasant cots were sometimes of improved workmanship and materials. At Wharram Percy in Yorkshire stone began to be used in the fourteenth century where timber, and earlier still turf, had furnished the previous walls. Something of the

90. *The Wealden type house in Willingham, which was destroyed by fire.*

nature of the later, more sophisticated, medieval houses of this type can be seen in the Black Houses of the Highlands and the Hebrides. Here the house is divided into two rooms, one for people and one for the beasts, with a common entrance. It is this feature, where associated with two opposed doors and a through passage dividing the byre from the house, that characterised the early 'longhouse' tradition in England. At the same time there appeared small cruck-built, open-hall houses, much smaller than the fully developed box-framed, open-hall houses of the South-East [91]. As with open hall houses and longhouses, they were divided in two by through passages with opposed doors. But there was a great difference between the longhouse, where the lower room was for animals, and the hall with its screens passage through which the pantry and buttery were reached.

Getting rid of smoke. The association of these stone-clad former open halls, both aisled and unaisled, of the West Riding with the sudden prosperity of the Yorkshire cloth industry certainly fits the achievement of a degree of comfort that they reached ahead of their contemporaries. From the first they appear to have eschewed the smoky open hearth on the floor of the hall for a smoke hood of timber and plaster. This, if shaped like a chimney, was wider and allowed enough space for seats underneath in the winter's cold.

In the South, smoke bays (which filled in the roof trusses on either side of a short bay to make it act as a chimney) and smoke hoods, appeared very late in the Middle Ages. Most houses eventually went straight to the chimney proper.

With the coming of the chimney, interesting arrangements were possible. In the South-East the stack was usually, although not always, inserted at the higher end of the hall, away from the through passage. Elsewhere it was often backing on to the passage, so that when a second hearth was added, back to back on the original, the passage was abolished.

Critical to rough-dating our houses at this stage, then, is the existence of aisles at some time or other, even if now abolished; the existence at some time of an open hall even if, as is most likely, a ceiling has been inserted; traces of a through passage, and the insertion of a chimney.

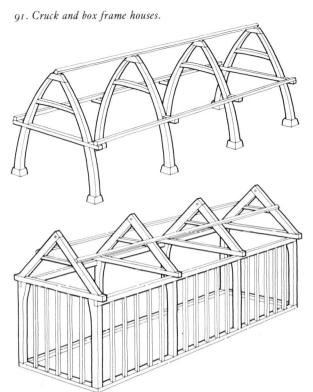

91. Cruck and box frame houses.

A useful starting point is Hoskins' 'The Re-Building of Rural England'.* In his article of this title Hoskins discovered from fieldwork and documents, especially Probate Inventories, that during the century 1540–1640, most of the houses in the English countryside were modernised or replaced. This had been reported by contemporaries like Rev. William Harrison, Vicar of Radwinter in Essex.** The oldest inhabitants of his village declared that the greatest changes in their lifetime had been 'The great multitude of chimneys of late erected', and other improvements in comfort, glass windows, and better furniture of all kinds. He later narrowed the period of his 'Re-Building' to 1560–1640. He knew well that there were harbingers before, and that some of the rebuilding had still to take place at the Restoration of Charles II, 1660. He knew also that it was concentrated into different periods, within the general span in different places.

*W. G. Hoskins *Provincial England*, Macmillan 1964. pp. 131–148.
**W. Harrison *A description of England*, 1577.

92. As we first found it, 21 High Street, was divided into two. In the nineteenth century the little cross wing that can be seen against the road, had been a shop and possibly a cottage as well. When we arrived it was a coal-shed. The front door opened where the screens passage had once been, and fixed screens to avoid draught had been installed on not very dissimilar lines.

93. 21 High Street today. This was an attempt to repair and restore what had survived, and when necessary to compromise to make it good to live in. We had no intention of restoring a fake open hall and screens passage. Anyway, the main tie beam of the hall had been cut.

21 High Street, Landbeach.

One of the perils of local history is that anyone who dabbles in it will take any opportunity to go over old houses that become empty. Quite a lot of these will come on the market. One may be restrained on one's own behalf but it may be too tempting for a spouse. Local history took me to 21 High Street; my wife saw that I bought it [92]. I was first introduced to it as a pair of cottages, and found great difficulty in distinguishing its type from outside. It had an axial chimney of the kind inserted or built so frequently in the two or three generations before the Civil War, but was this chimney between the second and third room, or was it in the middle of four? From the outside it looked as if there was an extra fourth room on the ground floor, but only three upstairs. Then there was a little cross-wing on the north; was it original or a later addition? It could be the most common type of pre-Civil War house, with three rooms down and three up, that had additions at each end. This raised a problem with the doors. The door on the south side, which was in two parts like a stable door, was not in the right place, alongside the chimney, for that type of house. However, on the north side I found a door opposite the chimney, even if it was fastened permanently shut.

But there were still nagging suspicions that I was missing the obvious. I was not following my own precept, to remember that a house has a history rather than a date. There were at least two eighteenth-century cottages in the village, much tinier than No. 21, and one

94. An earlier repairer saved what timbers he could on this more vulnerable north side, sawed them into more, if slighter struts, and replaced the rotten studs with them. The scarf joint in the rafter above, where the peg-holes show, testifies to the venerable age of the roof timbers.

of them so low that its attic was useless for accommodation so that, effectively, it was of one storey only. Were the upstairs rooms in No. 21 attics only?

When we first went inside, the only pieces of timber that we could see in the wall were at a place where it is now obvious that there had been major repairs and replacement in the eighteenth or even nineteenth century. Later we were to find that the work in the north wall was the only part of the whole structure that had been so repaired [94].

When we had bought the house and work started, clues, proofs and history began to emerge. The back-to-back open hearth which we felt should be below such an axial chimney, as we could see outside, must be in the space missing between the two cottages into which it had been divided. The measured plan showed this

95. *This is the living room, the former 'hall' of the house taken from the screens passage end. When we bought the house, boards and plaster covered the chimney piece. The ground floor has been restored, but the solar behind the chimney is now the dining room. The heavy beam at the top of the picture, the flat, sagging joists and all the fireplace were inserted in the 'Re-building'. This fireplace and chimney were offset against one side-wall, leaving space for both a little entrance porch and a turning newell staircase. These had both gone. In the more common type the front door opened into the porch with doors off right and left to hall and parlour, and the stair was on the opposite side of the stack.*

96. *The main beam in the lounge is clearly in its original
position. The broad chamfer and endstop suggest a seventeenth
century date for the conversion and insertion of the ceiling.
When you suspect that a house has had a ceiling inserted,
it is good to have decisive evidence. On the left is part of one
of three mullions from an unglazed window. These mullions
run up into the wall-plate (the horizontal timber on the top of
the wall), but have been cut off below when the remains of
the old window were blocked up, and a re-used one fixed.
Clearly the window had to be changed when the new ceiling
ran across the old mullions. The big timber on the right both
acts as a ceiling beam, and does the work of the tie-beam
now cut out in the room above. The wrought iron strap enables
it to hold the walls in, as a good tie-beam should.*

97. *Here the ends of the beam in the dining room show that
it is re-used. It has fifteenth-century mouldings which run right
into the pillar without an endstop.*

missing space to be nine feet or more each way.
Judicious rapping on the plaster and pressing on the
wallpaper confirmed the probable presence of two very
large open fireplaces, and the beam over the wider
hearth revealed heavy moulding suspiciously like one
common in the fifteenth century. The decision had to
be taken to go ahead in faith and open the hearths by
pulling away the twentieth century grates and the
cupboards at their sides. The hearths and chimney were
against the wall and rafters on one side, leaving room for
both stairs and baffle entry porch at the other side by the
door that had been nailed up. The exciting moulded
beam over the larger hearth was obviously re-used. It
had no end-stops where it went into the wall, and all
along it were the mortises where joists of fifteenth
century style had fitted in their former home.

The original turning newel had gone, and the landing
and rickety substitute stair connected only with the
back of the house. The other had been cut off by nailing
up the door, covering it with tongue and groove
boarding, and filling the space so formed with saw-dust
to deaden the sound. Beyond the stair a timber frame
covered with lath and plaster divided the house beside
the chimney. The house was beginning to emerge from
the disguises with which its history had covered it.

Even before the ceilings were pulled down we could
see the stout, oak ceiling beam in the principal room
downstairs [95]. Its wide chamfers and good end-stops
would fit with a seventeenth-century date [96]. It was
obviously in its original place as all four end-stops were
cut for its present position. But it ran across the room
from side to side rather than take the easier path under
the ridge, and it was tied in to the posts with wrought
iron straps. It appeared to be acting as tie-beam as well
as ceiling beam. One end of the massive timber beam
seemed to be resting on a light piece of wood nailed on
to the studs.

The other room with a fireplace [98] had a much
rougher beam that did run along under the ridge. One
end of this beam likewise resting on a very light piece of
wood fastened into oak with simple iron nails, and the
other end was propped on the beam over the hearth [99].
The joists on both sides where they reached the walls
were supported by rails of softwood nailed to the studs.
On the south side, the ends of the joists were extended by
tapered fillets, very characteristic of ceilings inserted in

98. *The brick pillar at the left of the fireplace in the modern dining room appears to be built of eighteenth century brick. This corner and only this one, was brought forward to make room for a bread oven, the black 'hole' on the left. The pillar and the beam across the open hearth had to be replaced to fit the new demands. This second hearth with its oven is much bigger then the other. The herringbone brick at the back is the commenest form of brick fireback. More expensive firebacks were usually made of cast iron and often had very ornate designs.*

a house whose walls were already standing.

Throughout the house the joists were all laid in the weakest way, resting on their broad sides instead of on their edges. This is typical of the old style before the eighteenth century. In the room against the road, where the joists are roughest, many still carrying bark, there were clear signs of a ladder-like stair in the corner [100]. This fits with the suggestion that this room was the first to be lofted over when the original house had been open to the rafters in every room, and at that stage was of one storey throughout.

When part of the inside of the thatch and rafters were temporarily exposed, they were heavy with soot. When the floor of the main room was excavated, a hearth of red and black burned earth was exposed. When the plaster was stripped from the inside of the walls to enable the timbers to be treated, the top half of an unglazed window with three diamond mullions running right up to the wall plate appeared [101]. The ceiling ran right across the window. The window clearly belonged to an early phase of the house before there was any ceiling. Sockets for a similar window, exactly opposite the first across the hearth, were also found.

In the large bedroom upstairs, immediately over the main room below, one can see where the tie-beam was

99. *(left) A more common way of inserting a ceiling and its beam is revealed in the dining room – which has a larger fire place. A rough timber, scarcely squared and chamfered with difficulty, has one end propped on the end of a short leg resting on the hearth beam.*

100. *Running out of the left-hand top corner of this picture is a joist of pine, set on edge in the modern fashion. This has been inserted to replace the support cut away from the adjacent joists, when the posts and ladder that had been fitted were taken away. Originally the top of the ladder would probably have been closed by a trap-door. This appears to have been the first part of the house to be lofted over.*

101. *In this room above the Hall, the top of the old medieval type window, and its three mullions, are still clearly visible on the left of the window. The beam supporting the ceiling can be seen downstairs in the lounge. (plate 95).*

cut away to make one big room without leaving a low hurdle right across the centre of the room [103]. This accounts for the peculiarities of the beam below which doubles as tie-beam.

When we came to look at the frame of the halved door, at the end of the cross passage, we found the mortise for a beam and its brace, part of the frame of the screen that at one time ran across the room to the door on the other side [104]. The main room downstairs would originally have been the hall, open to the rafters; the room next to the road through the screens passage would have been the servery where the food and drink were stored and prepared, although cooking would have taken place on the hearth in the hall. The servery would by this time here have almost certainly been called 'kitchen': and the original room, which now has the other hearth, would have been called the 'parlour' and

102. A view right through the first floor of the house. In the seventeenth century, and even later, corridors were dispensed with, and one had to move door by door from room to room.

used as a bedroom for the family. Servants would sleep in the hall.

The added room at the back has pit-sawn rafters, where the rest of the house makes do with rough poles with the snags knocked off with an adze, and its wall timbering on the ground floor is of eighteenth-century style. Additions like this were not uncommon, especially of dairies or sculleries. Peg holes in the inside of the original end wall have led one expert in vernacular housing to suggest that they were for warping pegs for setting up a loom. This accords well with the probable explanation of some of the peculiarities of the little cross-wing. This has a let-down shop shutter which was the earlier one of a pair running almost the whole length of the building [**105**]. Complete, it would have the appearance characteristic of a weaver's window. I have come across the inventory of a poor weaver in Landbeach, although I do not know where he lived. The cross-wing has a floor inserted, probably quite early in its life. Before this the open space would have been ideal for a vertical loom.

103. The main timber running straight across the picture is the wall-plate. The piece of wood resting on it is what is left of the tie-beam that was cut out to get rid of its obstruction to the bedroom. Underneath the tie-beam at the left are the diamond sockets for three mullions, matching those on the other side.

104. These timbers remain from the original front doorway. The primitive medieval hinge stone was found below it. The mortise is designed for the end of a horizontal beam, supported by a bracket, part of which is still in the slot below. This was part of the screen of the passageway from front door to back.

105. (right) The wooden shutter was once designed to let down as a shopcounter in medieval fashion, although it was much more recent than that. When it was all one window, it would look very much like a weaver's window to let in maximum light on a loom. The cross-wing may have begun life as a weaver's shed.

106. The plans show the three main stages in the history of the house. (a) A three-roomed house open to the roof throughout, a screens passage between hall and servery, and hearth on the floor in the centre of the hall between two tall unglazed windows. (b) The Great Re-Building. The addition of two back-to-back fireplaces with a chimney enables all rooms to be ceiled over and the three rooms become six. (c) Two major modifications which appear to date from the eighteenth century were the addition of the cross-wing (weaver's shed or shop?), and the lean-to at the back, probably a dairy. Both were originally of one storey only, and the dairy addition only acquired a ceiling with a bedroom above early in this century.

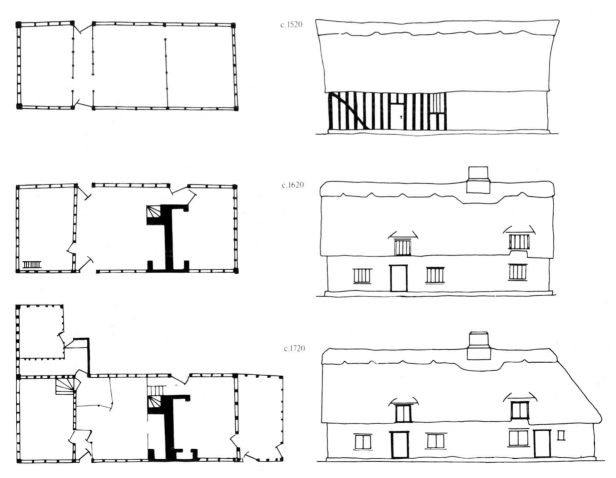

c.1520

c.1620

c.1720

The shop never had any direct connection with the house; in fact there was an empty passage between them, whose purpose is difficult to see unless it were to deaden the noise of something like a loom.

We have thus something like a history of the house from archaeological evidence: it was built as a three-roomed open-hall house with a cross passage. Even in the remotest part of the Fens this style was not built after 1540 [106].

The insertion of floors, hearths and chimney are part of the common modernisation that Hoskins referred to as the 'Re-Building of Rural England'. In Cambridgeshire this took place mostly a generation or so either side of 1620, and in most cases before the Civil War.

The next major change seems to have been the addition of the rooms which we conjectured as dairy and possible weavers' shed. About the same time there was an alteration to the bigger of the two fireplaces. One of the pillars has been rebuilt in later brick of the eighteenth century. At the same time that end of the hearth has been brought eighteen inches forward, to make room for the bread oven, which is still there. This necessitated rebuilding the hood with a longer beam. Presumably the fifteenth-century ceiling beam was put in this place at that time.

Time passed, and instead of further improvements, the house was split into two in the nineteenth century, and the shop may have acted as a one-up one-down house also, since it was fitted with one of the little square chimneys like those so often put on the gable of old houses to enable another family to be crammed in.

More interesting than the history of the alterations to the structure would be the stories of the people who lived here. So far I have only made a start in collecting these. Eyewitnesses have taken me back to what it was like living in it at the beginning of this century.

The Field Book of 1549 makes it quite clear that Nicholas Aunger lived here then. It so happens that no less than two wills of a man of that name survive. The pious bequests look after the community as well as children, godchildren and servants. One wonders why the silver spoons in the will of 1551 are not in that of 1555, but somehow they are missed less than 'my little red cow with the white face' who brought the whole to life. Most of all, when it came in 1549 to a question of who would withstand the petty tyrant of the fields of Landbeach, it is good to find Nicholas Aunger's name heading the charge. His family had been on the brink of rising socially in other parts of Cambridgeshire since the thirteenth century at least. I am glad that he had not risen too far by 1549.*

The start of modern houses. If the dropping of the aisles is the first symbol of major change in house patterns in the Middle Ages, the coming of the chimney marks their end and the beginning of modern times. The early sixteenth century, up to about its mid-point, shows the beginning of change in fashions which were soon dropped for more satisfactory ones. In this early phase chimneys were often placed on the long side of the hall, on the outside of the house, with only the hearth and hood coming through the wall. The other feature which enables some of these early houses of the 'Re-Building' to be picked out is the continuous *jetty*. This shows that the hall range is two-storeyed from the start, jetties being carried on the ends of joists. Earlier open hall houses had most often been jettied at the cross-wings, but after the coming of the chimney jetties soon fell from favour – at least, in the countryside. Fairly soon, in timber-framed houses, the axial chimney [108], which could heat two rooms with back-to-back hearths, and whose lost heat would all go into the house instead of the air round about, established itself as almost universal where houses were timber-framed. There were a few gable-end chimneys of this period, but they were *very* few, are hard to recognise, and mostly to be found with the smaller one- or two-celled houses that are relatively rare in the South-East.

The dominant type of house in the area where the 'Re-Building' went furthest and first, was the three-celled, either in the double-fronted form or the form with three cells in line.

The houses of the period of the 'Re-Building' nearly always have features very recognisable from the outside, once you get used to them, but nothing can be asserted very firmly from external evidence alone. The most obvious external feature of this period is the axial chimney running along the ridge. Back-to-back open hearths heated two rooms – the hall (living-room/kitchen) and parlour (bedroom) – and from them

*J. R. Ravensdale, 'Landbeach in 1549', *loc. cit.*

107. The beginning and the end of post-medieval vernacular styles. In the foreground, the continuous jetty – a harbinger of the 'Re-building', and two doors away the gable-end chimneys that remain common from the eighteenth century.

emerged the square flues side by side through the ridge – resulting in this very characteristic shape. The door is opposite the chimney, and opens into a little porch (baffle entry) with a door on one side to the parlour, and one on the other to the hall. On the far side of the chimney there is often what looks like a cupboard door, which opens to reveal the turning newel staircase.

The windows show clearly that there are three rooms downstairs and three rooms upstairs in the most common type in south-east England. In some of the meaner versions, especially where older houses of only one and a half storeys were being modernised, either or both the end upstairs windows may be in the gable end. Alongside this dominant type the two-celled and the rare four-celled (if there ever was such and not a pair of semi-detached) form a family. This family is paralleled to some extent by descendants of the hall and cross-wing types. The three or two units of hall, service and parlour can be arranged in a variety of shapes: L, T, H or E, and in spite of popular myths about H being for Henry VIII, and E being for Elizabeth I, they have no chronological significance.

Older hall houses that have been modernised tend to give themselves away. Aisled halls that have had their aisles removed may show this in the length that the cross-wings project. In general, the older the house the less the three units appear to have been designed together. In the oldest houses of this sort, the cross-wings do not match for size, and eaves and ridges run at different heights. This is less so in the aisleless open hall than in its predecessor, and in the pseudo-hall (of two storeys) and cross-wings of the later sixteenth and early seventeenth centuries the three units tend to be quite congruent. Double-fronted houses like this continued to be built from time to time even in the eighteenth century, but these late examples tend to give themselves away by a centrally placed door in a symmetrical façade. This coming of the quest for symmetry, to which medieval man seems to have been completely immune, marks the end of vernacular style in English architecture, or, at least the beginning of the end.

Away from the South-East the three-cell house was much less dominant, and in the South-West single-cell two storey houses were being built on the moorland in the late eighteenth century. In Devon the classic long-house, with (by contrast with the early longhouses that has ceased to be built a century before), two storeys in the house-part, flourished for about a century up to 1700. As they faded in Devon so they appeared in large numbers in the North-West.

One of the ways of showing symmetry in the design of a small house is to move the chimney to the gable-ends and separate the back-to-back hearths, one to each end. This fits with the changes of walling to brick and stone. It is typical of eighteenth-century cottages in the South-East. For a short time between the two styles the Queen Anne chimney was common – an axial chimney, square in plan, and usually very large.

There were two ways commonly used later in the history of the vernacular house to increase the room. Where it was living-space that was needed, the parlour end was doubled, with the result often that it looked like a cross-wing. Where service room was wanted, a common practice was to add an outshut, a lean-to along part or whole of the rear wall. The result can sometimes be mistaken for an aisle.

When a farmhouse reached the size of a three-celled house with both an enlarged parlour and an outshut, it was meeting needs that perhaps could be better met by a double-pile house. In these the whole house was now

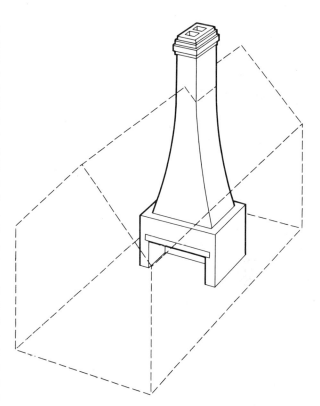

108. Axial chimney typical of the 'Re-Building' period in the century before the Civil War.

two rooms deep, and there was a division between the family's rooms on the one hand, and the service and servants area at the rear, on the other. Each had their own staircase – the grand one in front and the mean one for the servants in the rear. From the middle of the eighteenth century this became the almost universal farmhouse pattern.

Sometimes direct description of past housing survives. Surveys of estates occasionally contain details of housing covering a large number of houses over a wide area. One class, parsonages, is particularly well served. Glebe terriers (and these survive in diocesan archives in large numbers from the seventeenth and eighteenth centuries), can sometimes give very detailed descriptions of parsonage houses, even including the barns and the outhouses and their uses. But the greatest source is a document that survives in vast numbers.

The probate inventory. In 1538 it became necessary to produce an inventory drawn up by two honest neighbours of all a dead man's belongings before probate could be granted of his will, or before Letters of Administration could be granted to the heirs where there was no will. Often the appraisers went round systematically room by room, recording everything one room at a time. Where an inventory is specific as to which room the articles are found in, it virtually gives us a snapshot of the interior of the house on a particular day. With care, and some knowledge of the local patterns of houses, it is often possible to derive the type of house, including the use of each room from the inventory. It may also be possible to watch a family's most prized possessions and housing through several generations. It would be a pity to go through the mass of local inventories simply to track house types. They contain so much material on the past of ordinary people, frequently taking us around the peasant's farmyard and the crops in his fields, as well as his home.

The decline of vernacular housing. The eighteenth-century cottages, semi-detached, with gable-end chimneys, and front door usually opening into the living-room, represent a marked falling off in standards from the houses of the small peasant of the seventeenth century. As the new, meaner type of accomodation for the poor was introduced when population pressure grew acute in the eighteenth century, the old vernacular houses were nearly always modified to take in more labourers' families. A two-, three-, or four-celled house could be split into two without building another chimney, on the line of the back-to-back hearth. To split the three- or four-celled house further then required one or two more flues, and in house after house one can see where these were added in the form of small square brick stacks at the gables. Often the subsequent removal of these chimneys when the one-up one-down cottages to which they had been reduced were reunited is also very easy to see.

These housing developments might perhaps be described as a parallel to the contemporary developments in the industrial towns, the working-class housing perpetrated in the new towns in the Industrial Revolution. The vernacular cottage of the countryside, reduced by splitting to the lowest possible size of housing unit (even by the standard of those times), has its own social correspondence with the back-to-back or with the through-terrace housing of the cramped period of the Industrial Revolution. There is great scope for studying this sort of relationship and the generation of rural slums alongside industrial ones.

In looking at the massive Victorian development of towns, what the historian has to do is to discover what prevented expansion from simply spilling out in ever-widening circles. In the first place there were topographical and man-made restrictions, often the shape of the old open-field ways, roads and ditches, which hindered development. Then there are the motives and needs of the landlords, and their decision to sell, to develop or to hold off. The death of a lord of a manor in Cambridge, coming before all the procedures of enclosure of the Barnwell Fields was carried through, meant that his executors had to unload land for development. The result is many of the apparent peculiarities in the dates of adjacent patches of development, and until very recently complex social zoning. In Cambridge the even more peculiar needs of the University and colleges increased the demand for upper-middle class family houses once Fellows were allowed to retain their college fellowships on marriage. Other urban industries will show their own impacts on local development.*

*C. C. Taylor *The Cambridgeshire landscape*, Hodder and Stoughton 1973.

7 Parish Churches and Religious Houses

In any locality in England the chances are very high that the oldest building will be the parish church. As with vernacular houses, the commonest form for barn and church in the thirteenth century was also the aisled hall. Barns were sometimes built in this form as late as the nineteenth century, although aisles tended to disappear as time went by. In houses, the aisleless hall succeeded the aisled one as the dominant house type.

With the church the change came by breaking the pitch of the roof along the line of the aisle arcade. The roof over the nave was then reduced in pitch, often by lowering the ridge, and sometimes heightening the wall over the aisle arcades to allow a clerestory (a row of top windows to light the nave) to be inserted [**109**]. This left the water-table behind (the projecting line of chamfered stone intended to throw the rainwater away from the join between the roof and tower wall). This is nearly always pointed out to visitors as a sign that the church was once thatched; it may very well have been, since the low-pitched roofs of the fourteenth century would not have been possible without the use of lead as a cover, and not only would too much expensive lead have been needed on a steep pitch, but its weight would also have thrown a dangerous stress on the walls. Where the ridge was not lowered but, instead, the wall built up above the arcades to insert a *clerestory*, the water-table of the earlier roof sometimes is visible from inside, under the plaster on the tower below the nave roof. No one tries to explain this as the product of former thatching.

At the same time as the ridge was lowered, the aisles were usually widened. From being mere structural supports, or at best a processional way, the wider aisle in the parish churches could accommodate chapels and subsidiary altars, or monuments, much as monastic and cathedral churches were able to do on a larger scale.

Let there be light. If we think of the changing plan, and try to see what this implies in changing function, we suddenly leap forward in our understanding of medieval man. The windows of the thirteenth-century church and its predecessors were few and narrow, letting in little rain and, in spite of their splays, not

much more light. What light there was was concentrated at the east end over the high altar where the drama of Mass was enacted. The congregation would be in darkness in the ill-lit nave, an audience whose attention was focused by light on the action in the same sort of fashion as in a modern theatre. One difference would be that it was a 'promenade' performance with no seating.

The later Middle Ages saw the increase of light throughout the building, with cheaper glass and larger windows. Under the influence of the mendicant preaching orders, more churches became simple rectangular preaching halls. But in the same period the guilds developed in country as well as town. Their chapels and chantries brought the Mass closer to the people, *Easter Sepulchres* and Corpus Christi processions involved laity as well as priests in new dramatic teaching. But at the same time the development and elaboration of the wooden rood screens divided the order of priest from the order of laity once more, with the sanctuary a Holy of Holies.

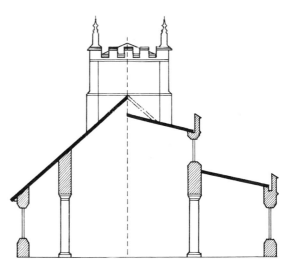

109. From the fourteenth century on, many parish churches were re-roofed with lower pitch and wider aisles. The use of lead for roof covering and more glass in larger windows and clerestory made for spacious, light interiors.

The feature which we still miss most of all from the late medieval church is colour. In only a few churches does the coloured glass survive, as in St Neot in Cornwall. Hidden from religious vandals in a cleft in the granite moor, the whole church interior is set ablaze as the sun streams through. Elsewhere a few fragments remain. Of the wall paintings less still survive, mostly patches of under-painting and these almost faded away.

Laity and the lay rector. With the institution of fixed seating, for a moment in the late Middle Ages, we can know a little of the images that made up the mind of the country carpenter, which he so tellingly carved on the pew-ends. He took his next-door neighbours as well as the creatures of his dreams to illustrate the Cardinal Virtues or the Seven Deadly Sins. Here, too, the mason who had become a fluent sculptor joined him. On the Seven Sacrament Fonts of the fifteenth century we can see the people and the sacraments alive: the old man on his death bed receives Extreme Unction, while under his bed can be seen not merely his slippers but also the used chamber pot [110].

Perhaps the most serious losses from the parish churches at the hands of the fanatics of the sixteenth and seventeenth centuries and the restorers of the eighteenth century were the painted sculptures of saints. The empty niches for these are a feature which hints, by the delicacy of the carving, at the quality of what has gone.

Visiting many parish churches, one becomes very much aware that the most frequent artefacts that remain from Queen Elizabeth's reign are the silver chalice and patten for the Communion. The most common survival from the acquisitions of the church around 1600 are the Communion rails set up on the instructions of Archbishop Laud, and the Elizabethan or Jacobean pulpits, often originally three-deckers. This probably has historical significance, but it is not quite so easy to say what is the reason for the survival of so many biers from this period.

In the eighteenth century changes in the arrangement of the church, and enormous increase in population and so of potential congregations, caused galleries to be built, making the interiors more like contemporary theatres. New churches of the period (as in Wren's London churches) adopted this plan from the start. At the same time high box pews were introduced to give the wealthier sections of the congregation a little privacy and freedom from draughts. For some squires who were also lay rectors (owners of the Great Tithes) a family box pew in the chancel, entered by a private lay rector's door, was private enough with stove and upholstered seating for family snacks during service.

The right of the lay rector to the chancel can still be used. I remember a church in which the sign that the service was about to begin was the local farmer's wife clattering in at the west door, and marching up to the chancel in her tweeds, with silver fox stole swishing and a rake to the grey felt hat. Her husband's land made him lay rector, and she exercised the rights more frequently than he did.

The reason that so many rectors were laymen after the Dissolution of the Monasteries was that the process of appropriation had allowed tithes in the Middle Ages to be diverted from parish churches to the support of monasteries. At the Dissolution, appropriated tithes would be seized by the king, and sold off or granted to laymen as income.

Memorials. Inside the church memorials give leads to village society in the past, and war memorials are perhaps the most eloquent of all. One does not otherwise find marble memorials to village labourers on the walls any more than one finds brasses to medieval villeins. Outside, in the churchyard, the common resting-place, one might expect more equality, but in medieval times the higher society often managed to be interred inside the church walls.

Out in the churchyard one suspects some much later social differentiation in the elaboration of the tombstones. It might be worth while for a local historian to investigate this, since one of the problems as to how

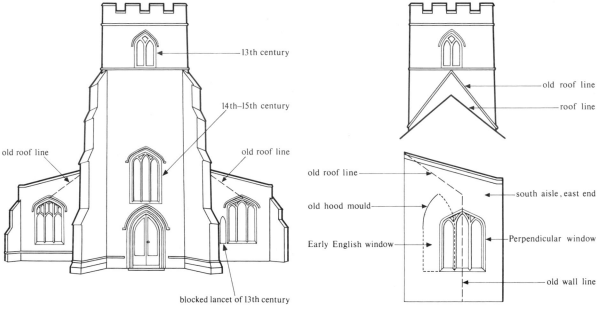

111. The west entrance of Oakington Parish Church, and (right) the tower from the east side and the interior of the south aisle facing east, as indicated from fragments.

much one can trust figures derived from gravestones is the degree to which they are representative of the whole population. Gravestones may well give information that appears in no other source. Sometimes they show relationships , or information on places of origin where weddings of village people have taken place outside the parish. But used alone, the information on gravestones must be handled with care. Hints of enormous infantile mortality in certain times and places may prove well-founded on investigation in more complete sources, but they should be checked.

Dates and history. The rough drawing of a church near where I used to live can show how simple, odd things noticed over a period soon add up to a perception of the church in its period of greatest glory [111]. The belfry window dates from the late thirteenth or early fourteenth century. The window below it is from the late fourteenth or early fifteenth century, and the door is fifteenth century, as are the two large windows at the west end of the aisles. So far the dating is from the shape

of the arches and window tracery, supplemented by the pattern of the mouldings. The battlements and the buttresses are also from the fourteenth or fifteenth century: earlier corner buttresses would have been in pairs, projecting in line with the main walls at right angles to each other.

Here, then, we have a fine example of the dictum that a church has a history rather than a date [112]. The evidence, with the tower windows getting earlier as one moves upwards, suggests an early fourteenth-century tower rebuilt in the fifteenth century, with perhaps a grand west doorway inserted in the lower stage of the tower at a later date still. There is other evidence clearly visible on this western exterior. In the west wall of the south aisle, close to the line of the aisle arcade, is a blocked up narrow lancet window [113]. This was obviously the west window of an earlier thirteenth-century aisle, very much narrower than the fourteenth-century one which

112. Oakington Parish Church. A splendid example of how a church has a history rather than a date.

113. The blocked lancet window belongs to the narrow aisle of the earlier thirteenth-century church. It was blocked when it was replaced by the bigger perpendicular window on the right, set in the centre of the wider aisle of that period. The stone's surface has been 'pecked' to provide a key for the plaster that would have hidden it.

appears today. Much harder to see, but quite clear once they have been made out, are two other tell-tale lines. These are the lines of the old aisle roofs, and they show up rather like a straight joint in brickwork, except that they run diagonally [114]. The wall here is of large flint pebbles, and when the fourteenth-century builder has extended the walls to widen the aisles, he has built out from the old wall without perfectly and invisibly bonding his work in.

There is further visual evidence to confirm this. If we go to the east beyond the chancel and look at the roof line where it abuts the tower wall, the water-table of the earlier, pre-perpendicular roof is still there above the present roof and is much steeper. This church offers a good example of what we described as a very common feature in the history of parish churches, the lowering and dividing of the roof pitch, when lead became available to make very low-pitched roofs.

In the interior are more confirmatory clues. If we go behind the organ and look at the eastern end of the south aisle, here we find a large perpendicular window occupying much of the space of the end wall. On the wall to the left and above the present window is a fragment of a hood mould of thirteenth-century date, apparently part of a two-centred arch which would fit the same period. This would seem to belong to the former east window of a narrow thirteenth-century aisle. To the right, in the south wall, is a simple double piscina. These can be dated to the reign of Edward I (1272–1307), and this one would have belonged to an altar in front of the window whose hood-mould remains. It must have been moved out to its present position when the aisle was widened in the fourteenth century. One of the important reasons for widening the aisles was to provide more room for side-altars and subsidiary chapels. There are two niches in the east end of the north aisle for later images of saints. The chapel with the double piscina and the big east window was probably the original Lady Chapel.

These few simple clues make it possible to reconstruct the pattern of the thirteenth century church, the barn-like structure, the interior full of gloom with its tiny lancet windows, except for light through the bigger windows in the chancel. We can also see something of how, and perhaps even a little of why, the building changed to match the needs of liturgical fashion. It is this kind of reconstruction and understanding which is the end of our study: the dating of detail is the means. Nevertheless, the pursuit, the perception of clues, and recognition of pattern has its own excitements and, needless to say, pleasures.

114. The east side of the tower clearly shows the line of the pre-Perpendicular roof which covered nave and aisle in a steep unbroken pitch.

The Fabric of Parish Churches

Dating features of medieval churches is something we can learn from practice with the help of a good book. The good books are numerous, and one of the latest and best is Richard Foster's *Discovering English Churches*.

At first we find how the shape of arches and window tracery give us an idea of their general period. Saxon and Norman used the round arch. After about 1180 this is replaced by the first pointed Gothic Order, the Early English with its sharp lancet windows.

A few years before 1300, lesser changes came to a climax with the appearance of the Ogee [116] in the tracery, and sometimes in the shape of the arch itself. This Ogee, the curve that runs back on itself like an 'S' or a backwards (S), becomes a special feature of the Decorated Style which lasts almost until the appearance of Black Death in 1349 halts major building for years. The Gatehouse of the Abbey at Bury St Edmunds was finished in 1347. Here you can see the Decorated style in its final perfection giving way to the first phase of the Perpendicular. This had just been imported from the Continent, but it died at home just as it became dominant in England.

The commonest type of arch in Perpendicular work is four centred, and tends to get flatter as time goes by. In window tracery its signature is the mullions (vertical bars) running right through to the arch.

Saxon church building has many features which separate it from all others. The use of long and short work at the corners, the use of stone turned on a lathe for shafts for small windows, double splay on windows, through stones for arches, low-relief sculpture of distinctive style, and many more. As you find and identify fragments of Saxon work with the help of the guide book, they will become very easily recognisable.

Ornamental features [118] can sometimes be precise in dating within a period, or may merely mark an overlap. There is, for example, a transition between late Norman and Early English in which decorative forms like nailhead are found in both, but most of the many Norman ornaments are peculiar to that style.

In Early English Dog-Tooth proliferates. The Ball flower and the Four leaved flower are pure Decorated as the so-called Tudor flower is Perpendicular, although it has its own Square flower as well.

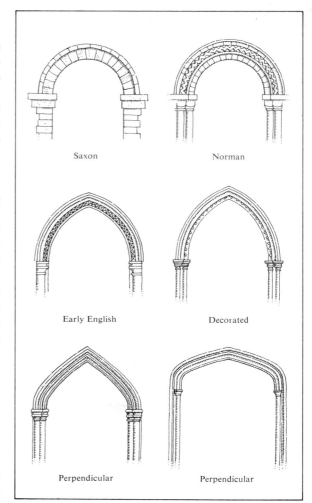

Saxon   Norman

Early English   Decorated

Perpendicular   Perpendicular

115. Some types of arch.

116. An Ogee.

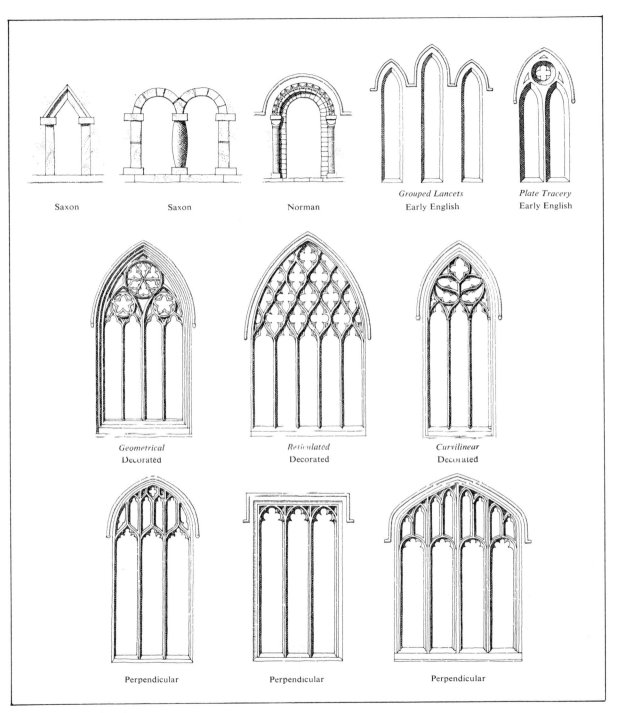

Saxon

Saxon

Norman

Grouped Lancets
Early English

Plate Tracery
Early English

Geometrical
Decorated

Reticulated
Decorated

Curvilinear
Decorated

Perpendicular

Perpendicular

Perpendicular

117. Some types of window.

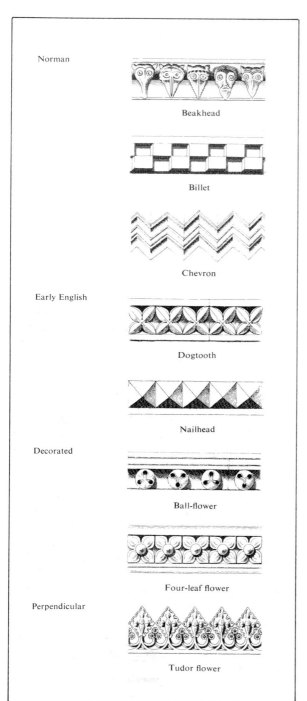

Norman

Beakhead

Billet

Chevron

Early English

Dogtooth

Nailhead

Decorated

Ball-flower

Four-leaf flower

Perpendicular

Tudor flower

118. Ornamental features.

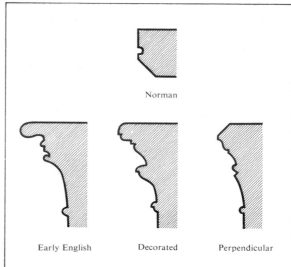

Norman

Early English   Decorated   Perpendicular

119. Mouldings.

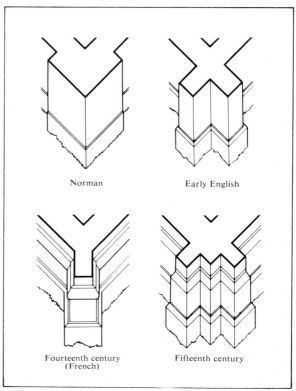

Norman   Early English

Fourteenth century (French)   Fifteenth century

120. Buttresses.

Mouldings [119] are probably the best and safest source for dating. In a Norman building, for instance, it may be possible to distinguish between early and late by whether there is a plain roll moulding or a keel moulding, that is one where the two halves come together like the keel of a ship.

Another very useful pair of mouldings change over in this way in the second half of the thirteenth century, and show up well as the base of columns. The earlier had deeply undercut hollows known for obvious reasons as 'water-holding' mouldings, made by exuberant use of the chisel. They were replaced by a simpler triple roll with three convex curves.

Elaborate mouldings can be dated by sketching a section of it to compare with the dated examples in H. Forrester's *Medieval Gothic Mouldings*. But four types of moulding are usually sufficient for matching the top of a column from which the arch springs, or a string-course which can date the whole wall. This is the projecting band of stone on the surface of the wall, and its moulding is usually simple and standard.

Buttresses [120], particularly at corners of buildings, can be very helpful. Just east of the Cathedral in Norwich a fragment of rough masonry foundation is enough to tell of the vanished thirteenth century Lady Chapel.

Tool-marks made in dressing the stone help surprisingly often, considering how limited this source is. Early Norman and Saxon stones show rough diagonal tool-marks from where they were dressed with the axe.

All this is a beginning. We need to fill the building with the people, and see it as a social institution.

Monasteries and Religious Houses

There can be very few places in this country that were not affected by the nearness of monasteries or religious houses before the Reformation. Those that escaped physical nearness probably were involved through some religious house owning property in the locality. One of the best ways of learning a great deal about a local religious house is to start from the standard Benedictine plan, and try to explain all deviations from this in any local example. The standard Benedictine plan evolved in practice so that plan fitted function. The working of the monastery could easily be depicted by flow-diagrams. In spite of our imagining medieval monasteries as romantic extravagances, they were probably as functional in their lay-out as any type of building from any era. Even the infirmary windows looked out over the monks' graveyard.

The deviations from the standard plan could simply be due to difficulties of the site. When the Cistercians went off into the foot-hills of the mountains, they sometimes could not even keep the east–west alignment for the church. Unlike the monks, the friars placed the emphasis of their work not on withdrawal from the world but on going out into the world to convert it. So they built their houses with churches that were preaching halls in the towns, fitting them in to what sites they could find, compromising with the problems of awkward shapes in built-up areas. They added further specialities of their own, like lecture halls and libraries, for the higher education of their brethren who were to become the intellectual élite and convert those suffering from ignorance, heresy or heathen beliefs all over the world.

However, differences in plan could also be an ideological matter. This was notoriously so when the Cistercian Order was founded in opposition to the laxity of the Benedictines, in the name of a return to the purity of the rule. So too was the development much later of a new order of Carthusian houses as virtually collective hermitages.

The other sort of deviation from the standard plan is not unconnected with the problems just mentioned of success, riches and corruption coming to each order in turn, except for the incorruptible Carthusians.

The converse of the reforming zeal with which each new order is founded is the softness and the comfort-loving latter days when they become once more deeply involved with the world. The precincts of many great Cistercian abbeys became markets for the wool-clip, and the abbeys themselves became financial institutions. This sort of change can be simply illustrated from the ruins of some houses. In the last days of Castle Acre Priory in Norfolk [121], the ruins show that building expenditure was lavished on the west range, especially the prior's rooms, and on the gate-house, where the outside world met the monastic house. The

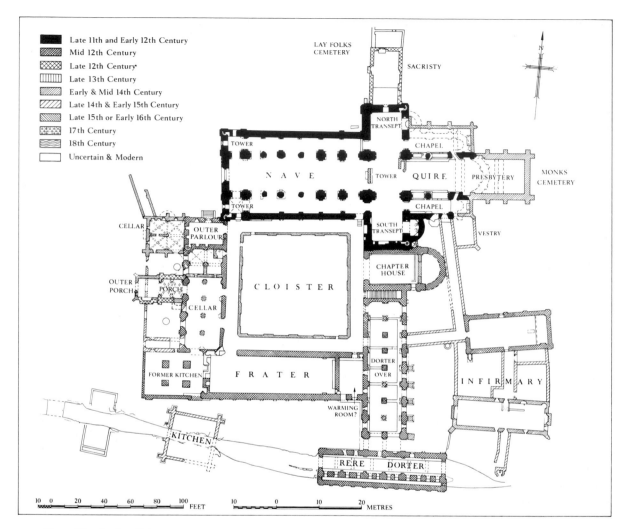

LAY FOLKS CEMETERY

SACRISTY

N

NORTH TRANSEPT

TOWER

CHAPEL

N A V E

TOWER

QUIRE

PRESBYTERY

MONKS CEMETERY

CELLAR

OUTER PARLOUR

TOWER

CHAPEL

SOUTH TRANSEPT

VESTRY

OUTER PORCH

PORCH

CLOISTER

CHAPTER HOUSE

CELLAR

FORMER KITCHEN

F R A T E R

DORTER

OVER

I N F I R M A R Y

WARMING ROOM?

KITCHEN

RERE DORTER

10 0   20   40   60   80   100   FEET   10   0   10   20   METRES

121. Plan of Castle Acre Priory.

prior seems to have become a rich man of the world rather than a man of God. The rest of the buildings were decaying and the brothers moved across for most purposes to the west range.

The next thing that the local historians with a monastery's ruins, or even more, a monastery converted into a great house, will want to investigate is the story of what happened to it at the Dissolution of the Monasteries. In nearly every county now the best starting point for such a story, and for the outlines of its

life as a monastery, will be the section on Religious Houses in their *Victoria County History*.

Nonconformity. No local history will be adequate if its fails to deal with the story of the local Nonconformists and their chapels. The buildings alone are a major note in the landscape. Their records, like their literature, are very much concerned with the journey of the soul. In their refusal to be dependent on squire and parson, they carried their opposition into life after death, by setting up their own burial grounds and escaping the parson's fee. In the countryside, the first such burial ground outside the churchyard very often belonged to the Quakers. They are sometimes extremely difficult to track down.

Nonconformist religion was highly charged with feeling, and their quarrels and schisms may be astonishingly well reported in their own records. A good deal may be discovered about the early growth of Nonconformity from the Archdeacon's Visitation Records. There is also an enormous amount of supportive social material in this early modern period, and as a result we can perhaps come to know many ordinary people better than at any time previously. Dr Margaret Spufford[†] has brought back whole communities of people who seemed gone for ever from this world. My favourite from her gallery is a charlady from the village of Over, Sister Sneezeby. In 1654 she was in grave danger of lapsing as a General Baptist, corrupted by reading Quaker pamphlets. When the Messengers visited her she was prepared to be reasonable, and listened, although this was perhaps not too demanding since she seems to have been rather deaf. But she went on reading, with the result that she was imprisoned later with other Quakers.

A rich harvest exists here for local historians. There is plenty in the study of the buildings of the chapels alone. Their earliest buildings were ones taken over from other uses, as houses, barns, or whatever was available. This was not at all objectionable to dissidents with a tradition of secret meetings at night, hidden in barns or still on horseback, ready to flee at a moment's notice. In the days when chapels had to acquire licences, one ruse was to build a pair of cottages and convert them before hostile potential objectors could become aware of what was going on. When, in more tolerant times, they came to build special chapels, the preaching theatre, with high pulpit, family box-pews and pine panelling, the general classical tone of churches like St Stephen Walbrook was there for the borrowing. Some impressive chapels, beautiful in their simplicity and with interiors not unworthy of the age of the Adam Brothers, survive from this early period. The early Methodist chapels in Cornwall were erected contemporaneously with the engine houses for the mines where their male congregations, and a good part

of the women, worked. Chapel and mine building managed to combine a simple rustic classicism that betokened their confidence. Billy Bray, the famous Cornish chapel builder, was a miner, and his tiny structures are as stark and simple as any mine buildings. This was the indigenous pattern, which in later times, with more spacious buildings, was reinforced by conscious imitation of Wesley's own churches, so leading back to the tradition stemming from Wren.

In Nonconformist chapels the battle of the styles in nineteenth century architecture could provide an outward and visible sign of inward and spiritual struggle by claim of status or assertion of difference. When there was a breakaway from the Baptist Chapel in Willingham, a beautiful, simple classic building, the dissidents built a large new Gothic church with rostrum, rails, Communion table and organ all set out in the new style. And the two glowered at each other across the road until the older, less comfortable, but simpler and more beautiful began to fall down. There is much to be discovered by examining the lively architectural life, as well as the spiritual life, of Nonconformist chapels.

The Religious Census. The chief source for attempting to discover the state of the Victorian Church is the notorious religious census of 1851.[*] Here again we come across the curious relation between religion and buildings. It is so much easier to discover facts about buildings that we are tempted to use the word church in the sense of building and forget the more elusive flock of souls and what was happening to them.

The census was an attempt to gather information about the support for both church and chapel. Clergy and ministers were asked to complete and return a form at the same time as the general census was taken. There was no compulsion, but where an incumbent refused, the enumerator tried to fill in the form on his behalf. It is reckoned that the Anglican Church was seriously under-recorded.

Unfortunately, the day chosen was Mothering Sunday when, traditionally, young men and women who were living away from home returned to their

*R. W. Ambler, 'The 1851 Census of religious worship,, *Local Historian*, vol 11, August 1975. pp. 375–81.

parents for the day with presents. The numbers of sittings are probably recorded more accurately than the attendances. In an age of intense rivalry between the established church and the Nonconformists, each side accused the other of inflating their figures. The bitterness engendered has prevented any agreement since then to hold another religious census.

One of the features of Church history in the nineteenth century is the building of new churches and chapels to cope with the swollen populations of new industrial towns and suburbs. It is possible to get help in following this from the census, which asked the date of erection for churches built since 1800. In areas covered by Ordnance Survey Town Plans (and it is unlikely to be required for villages where chapels will be few and their history probably known to their congregations), the churches will be shown with the number of sittings printed. Again the comparison of maps and plans for recent suburbs is one of the quickest and most efficient ways of building up a picture of growth.

8 Peopling the Landscape

All sorts and conditions. It is a common experience among those searching out local history that there are times when material being sorted into wheat and chaff produces an unconscionable proportion of chaff. There can be very few fields of historical research where this does not happen from time to time. It certainly applies in long, arid searches through the minutes of the Justices of the Peace in Quarter Session during the early modern period. The JPs in Quarter Session were the main organ of local government at the county level before the County Councils were set up. Among all the administrative business, and crime and punishment, there is all manner of licensing. Major roads and bridges dealt with by the county are recorded. The supervision of the Poor Law in the eighteenth century sometimes caused biographies of paupers and their movements to be taken down as evidence as to which parish was responsible for supporting this particular pauper. These provide a kind of information which can scarcely be found elsewhere: the annals of the poor are not only short and simple; they are mostly unrecorded.

Typical of the Quarter Sessions is licence of exemption for cottages built for the poor under the Cottage Act of 1589. In the case of the poor there was no need to provide four acres of field land if the Justices certified. For a brief time, at least, we can see something of the standard of the attempts to house the poor at this very early period. Sometimes the houses themselves can be clearly identified.

The total quantity of Quarter Sessions and County records is enormous: John Richardson, in his *The local historian's encyclopedia*, lists over fifty classes, and this work should be consulted.

A source which can prove of value to a local historian is the *Calendar of State Papers, Domestic*, and its predecessor, *Letters and Papers of Henry VIII*. The quantity of local detail that can be discovered here is very considerable. On subjects like the draining of the Fens, which involve petitions and counter-petitions from the tiniest communities, recognisable people start to move through the focus of the historian's view. We find a young Cromwell offering to delay the Drainers in the law-courts for 4d per head of the fenman's cattle.* He had recently been one of the signatories of petitions for concession for draining, but the King had moved in to take any profit for himself.

These *Calendar of State Papers* may be found in the big libraries. They are indexed and so can be used fruitfully and systematically for local history. The documents summarised in them are to be found in the Public Record Office, but the calendar entries are generous, and many give much useful information without going to the originals. Alternatively, they enable references to be prepared and documents to be ordered without wasting time in the Record Office.

National records. Such an enormous amount of resources for local historians is in the national collections that sooner or later one hopes to fit in a few visits. A little time in London can go a long way if the visit to the Public Record Office can be prepared beforehand. If access can be had locally to a big library which carries the sets of *Lists and Indexes of the Public Record Office*, then the hours of searching out the references need not eat up precious London time. A further saving can be made by the use of photo-copying facilities. London time can be almost exclusively devoted to inspecting and selecting potential material for reproduction. The work can then be done at home. The staff at the Public Record Office will help you in your efforts to make the best use of your time, and this is likely to become more important than ever under the new arrangements at the PRO.

Royal court records. A class of document full of riches for the local historian is to be found in the Exchequer records, Depositions taken by Commission at the PRO. These are statements produced in the localities by writing down answers made on oath before the justices. So here, for one of the very rare times, we hear the voice of the English peasant,

*Calendar of State Papers, Domestic, 1631–33, vol. CCXXX no. 51, quoted by Darby, *The draining of the fens*.

even if only in reply to question. Sometimes we can almost recognise the tone. There was one such case in Waterbeach, a Wordsworthian situation where an idiot mother had produced an idiot boy. He had been put into the vicar's care for 2s 6d per year, but the vicar had subcontracted him for 6d. One of the local inhabitants when asked whether he had always known the boy to be an idiot replied that he had always known him to be a simple man, 'but as to the word "idiot", he understood not what the word signifieth.' Reading these depositions produces an inescapable impression that the story of the unjust steward must have read as a scene from contemporary life in early modern England.

The records of the *Chancery* and the Royal Prerogative Courts are rich in local stories. The *Star Chamber* dealt only with cases in which violence was alleged, and so its records may need a little discounting on that score. In 1549 we find a group of our Landbeach peasantry 'in riotous manner arrayed, having upon them divers and sundry kinds of weapons, arrayed after the fashions and manner of war, that is to say with bills, bows, arrows, swords, daggers and other kinds of weapons'. In the event the only weapons we hear of these peasants having with them are crabtree staves with iron tines five or six inches long in them – that is, the sort of weapons giants carry in illustrations to fairy tales. But on the petitioner's side sword and dagger were used. A son-in-law, enclosing a piece of common, stabbed with his dagger a man who resisted.

Richard Kirby, the lord of the lesser of the two manors, had got rid of all his *copyhold* tenants and consolidated their homesteads into paddocks on which he could base enormous flocks and herds to exploit the common fens. He employed his sons-in-law and 'unhonest hired men' from other villages to terrorize the local peasants and keep them off the common as far as possible. He sat with drawn sword by the cross, guarding the gate of his land where the peasants' beasts were pounded. The degree of violence was getting very dangerous indeed, with seizure, impounding and rescue of beasts by both sides. The Rector, Matthew Parker, who was to be Queen Elizabeth's first Archbishop of Canterbury, seems to have intervened and restored peace, by backing the peasantry.

We next find Kirby at law with his sons-in-law. Male children would not survive for Kirby, and when he himself fell sick (the symptoms sound very like an early case of syphilis), the villagers thought a new private version of the plagues of Egypt were falling on him by divine dispensation. But failure of male heirs to survive meant that he had to marry off three daughters who would require land to endow them, but he would get no return to the family estates by marrying sons.

He passed his daughters off to nearby farmers at Huntingdon, Milton and Haddenham, by offering to secure to each the reversion of one-third of the manor and £40 cash on demand. As time went by it became increasingly obvious that Kirby had no intention of fulfilling his obligation: no deed conveying the reversion of the manor, nor any down payment appeared. One by one the sons-in-law took Kirby to court. He knew that it would pay both sides to come to an agreement out of court, and appears to have halted expensive processes by the simple expedient of coming to agreements he had no intention of honouring. He had tormented the peasants with vexatious litigation in his previous actions in the Royal Courts.

We next find Kirby petitioning in Chancery against his daughter Elizabeth and George Hasell, his son-in-law from Huntingdon. He describes himself as a widower, 'also then was and yet is impotent and lame and destitute as well of his hearing as of his speech'. He had given the whole order and rule of his house, and the whole order and rule of his goods to Elizabeth his daughter (typical of the man, he manages to put it as if he is doing his daughter a favour by allowing her to look after him). While Elizabeth stayed at Landbeach her husband came over from time to time, and stayed on for as much as a fortnight, sometimes for more, sometimes less. When George went home he never went empty-handed, but took with him a selection of his father-in-law's 'deeds and bonds, goods, chattels, napery and ready money to the value of one hundred pounds and better'. Hasell had two confederated with him in this affair, John Richardson and Robert Blinkinghorne, and Kirby could not find out where any of his missing goods were. Indeed he was not quite sure what was missing, or even what it looked like now, whether it was 'in bag or box, sealed or unsealed, or chest, locked or otherwise', nor did he know the precise value of what was missing.

As so often with the cases at the Royal Courts we have no record of the decision, merely the Bill and

Rejoinder, but a momentary appearance breaks surface in 1566. There in the parish register is the record of Kirby's marriage to Widow Margaret Meryall, and the note that he had to be carried to church in a chair to get married. If this was a last fling to try to prevent his sons-in-law getting their just deserts, it may have failed. Kirby died a few weeks later, and we do find evidence of his daughters inheriting their shares. But as regards the village, his death seems to have finally brought peace.

A fascinating and significant case in the Chancery is shown in a Petition from John Pepys of Cottenham, one of the relatives of the later diarist's family. Alice Harrison, a widow who had remarried, found herself with three other daughters to marry off, besides Edith Talbot, from a previous marriage. She 'moved and procured' John 'to become a suitor in marriage unto Edith'. After Alice perceived that John was 'in some towardness of a contract of matrimony with the said Edith', she tried to extract a promise from John that he would give her the £40 legacy left to Edith by her father, Edmund Talbot. Alice was the executrix of Edmund's will, and she and her husband still held the legacy. When John promised to give the legacy, her son persuaded her to refuse it and ask instead that John should give a bond to Alice for £40 and also secure on Edith for life some lands of which he held the copyhold in Cottenham. 'Whereupon, by subtle persuasion and enticement of the said Alice and Richard [Richard Skott, her son], the said Edith was conveyed into Northamptonshire, far from the dwelling of your oratour [John Pepys, the petitioner] and there kept close and hidden [from him] . . . whereby he was more troubled and driven to spend more money and a large time, seeking where to find, and how he might come to speak with the said Edith.'

In the end, worried with the loss of his time and the spending of his money, he gave way and promised to Alice what she asked. But she did not wish her husband to be 'privy or know her doing therein', and so arranged that the bonds should be made to Richard Skott and Baldwin Skott, his son. Yet notwithstanding all this, immediately 'after Pepys was bound . . .'

As so often in these cases, the lower end of the parchment is rubbed or damaged, and we feel a little like John Pepys. All the same, the case shows something of the operation of one of the most important parts of social life in the reign of the first Queen Elizabeth, the operation of the marriage and estate market among the yeomen and gentry.*

It might be worth pointing out that not all the Bills that came to the Royal Courts had dating evidence on them, and so they may be misplaced. For instance, in the Star Chamber Kirby's Bill against the peasants was filed in 1549 where it should be, but the reply to it was filed forty years earlier. When searching, it may be worth spreading the net a little wider than appears necessary. The records of the Royal Courts may not be the source easiest of access to local historians in that they involve visiting the Public Record Office, yet they are probably the best of all waters in which nets can be let down for a draught if they are in need of excitement for a story.

*Public Record Office, C3 136/29.

9 Informal Records

Place names. It is a paradox that our first literary source for the history of any place is likely to have come from an illiterate age, and to have been spoken only, and not written down for centuries. A high proportion of early place names contain an element from a man's personal name. This may be our only contact, unless archaeology can help, with the first identifiable settlers in any particular place. The absence of earlier evidence should not deceive us into thinking that there were no people there before our first names appear. Place names are like fingerprints in words: they are personal, positive, may prove a vital clue, but are limited in use unless they can be identified in a bank of examples, and are not indestructible.

The language from which so many of our old names comes can tell us something of the settlement and survival of peoples: Celtic and Latin from the Romano-Britons; Anglo Saxon, Old Danish and Old Norse from their successors.

Our understanding of place names has been undergoing a revolution. In the early nineteenth century, when German scholarship was being imported to English universities, the science of philology was applied to English place names. A large number were noticed which were formed of a personal name and the ending – *ingas*, meaning 'the people of' – for example, Hastings meaning 'of the people of Haesta'. Others might have an ending which implied a settlement, for instance *–ham* or *–ton*, meaning 'farm' or 'village'. At that time German historians' minds were full of ideas of the Folkwandering and of nomadic, unsettled agriculture, and, incredible as it now seems, the *–ingas* names were regarded as proof of the earliest types of invasion of Britain simply because they contained no habitation element. It seems strange to think of villages being known by non-place names.

Increasingly in recent years it became more and more obvious that the pagan Saxons, whose cemeteries were often being dated to the earliest phases of penetration, appeared to have little or no connection with villages that had *–ingas* names. Place-name scholars have put in an immense amount of research to clear up the confusion and redevelop the contribution of their studies to the history of settlement. Something more subtle, and we hope in the end more useful, seems to be emerging: *–ham*, especially in the form *–wicham*, seems generally to be very early, with *–ingaham* later, and *–ingas* and *–ing* later still. Topographical names which were once thought to be late and of little importance are now subject to intensive study. Names such as *–feld*, *–ley* and *–hurst*, implying clearances from woodland, are associated with the immense forest clearance during the Saxon period.

The commonest Saxon element in village names is the suffix *–ton* or *–tun*, meaning the same as *–ham*, a farm or village. It seems to occur over a wide time span, and can be very late indeed. It often appears with a directional element – for instance Sutton (South-tun) – and such names may well help us to understand the process whereby Saxon villages and parishes developed from the break-up of great estates, whose origins may in some cases run back into prehistory.

Scandinavian place names have held their own as indicators of Danish settlements, and close analysis with fieldwork is giving them even more meaning. A comparison between the site-quality of Danish and English villages in areas of dense Danish settlement suggests that Danes were far from taking over all the best sites, and most frequently fitted in between the settlements of Saxons who stayed on. Place names may sometime show where a Danish band took over. The so-called 'Grimston hybrids', where a Danish name is compounded with the Saxon suffix *–tun*, may represent this process, which now seems much less common than we once thought.

Current work on English place names, while a new, and perhaps more telling, if more complex, chronology is being built up, is most exciting. The Dark Ages are being penetrated by new shafts of light. Two very clear articles about these changes can be found in the *Local Historian*, both by Margaret Gelling: 'Recent work on English place-names', vol xi, no. 1, February 1974; and 'Topographical settlement names', vol. xii, no. 6, May 1977.

Minor place names, sites within a village, may have more to tell the local historian than the village name because there are so many more of them. Secondly, these lesser names may not have been so closely identified and examined by the expert, and so the amateur is thrown back more on his own resources. Because of a detailed, intimate knowledge of the area under study, the amateur may in fact in some measure be equipped to become the local expert. If the place name or the elements which constitute it is not in the county volume of the *English Place Name Society*, or if no volume has been published for the county, the amateur should try the *Oxford dictionary of English place-names*, by Ekwall.[†] If there is still no help from the experts, or if there is reason to doubt what is offered because of special local knowledge, range all the versions of the word in question according to the date of their appearance, in order to avoid being misled by late alterations, and try to work out the meanings of the earliest forms.

Oakington in Cambridgeshire provides a good example of such late alterations. Its ultimate origins seems to be drawn from a Saxon chief's name, Hucca. By the eighteenth century it had developed into Hogginton. This was offensive to the more substantial persons in the village, and so the name was modified.

The Waits. An interesting example of the sort of special problem the local historian may meet in dealing with place names came up in my work on the Fen Edge. In Cottenham there were a number of enquiries as to the meaning of the name, 'the Waits'. This at first appeared to be associated with a group of trees behind the old Rectory. Then it became obvious from some early nineteenth-century notes on it in a register of general information in the parish chest that it referred to a now dried up pond in the Rectory garden, which had a sunken path leading to it from the Cut, a former drainage ditch and canal. This looked for all the world like an old dock for the little, narrow fenland barges. Fortunately I later came across a reference in the 1450s to payment for the carriage of large stones from 'les Weightes'. It appeared to have been a name given to this dock, the former medieval deep-water dock, and, as mentioned above, there was reason to date it back at least to Norman times.

While this was going on I found the name in Landbeach, where it also referred to a dock, one that no longer exists, but which before being filled in was at the southern end of the Beach Lode. I was again lucky in finding an early mention of this in the middle of the fourteenth century – 'le Waygate'. Much more obvious and easy was finding the next example. Driving towards the bridge at St Ives, I looked up across the river, and there was a neat cast-iron street name on the side of a wharf, 'The Waits'. It then appeared that this word had some general meaning, either where cargo was weighed or boats waited (since it must have been single-line traffic in those narrow canals). It must be a remarkable coincidence that the old dock area at Ramsey, which was enormous by medieval standards, was called by the names 'the Great Whyte' and 'the Little Whyte', unless these were ultimately the same word.

The change to this form of the word was beautifully unfolded by driving north, alongside the culvert that now covers the Great Whyte and on into the fen. There I passed through what the map said was Ramsey Heights, admitted as a corruption of Ramsey 'Eyots' or 'Aits', having been given a polite form as happened in Oakington. The old name from before the Fens were drained is not so obviously significant when it takes a flood to reveal the old islands; before the Great Draining the islets would have been cut off each winter by the black water. The change in pronunciation from 'Waits' to 'Whytes' is an example of the common medieval process known as the Great Vowel Shift.

Folk tales. As well as such history as we can find in the language of place names, there is as much and more in folk memories, a great deal more in straightforward memories of social life and conditions from the past two generations, and yet still more in myth and folk-tale that have encapsulated hidden meanings. These latter may deal in very old happenings.

In the story of the Devil or the aborigines moving the stones when the church of Cottenham was being rebuilt, there is good reason to believe that this tale, referred back to an event of the Norman period (see page 69).

A similar story occurs in several towns which have late medieval bridges. The version at Wadebridge in Cornwall attributes, quite correctly, its building to

John Lovibond, a fifteenth-century Vicar of Egloshayle on the opposite bank of river. According to the legend, Lovibond's first efforts were frustrated by sinking foundations, which were invariably swallowed up in shifting sands. However, it was revealed to him in a dream that he should first place bales of wool as foundations, and then all would be well. He did, and all was well (I hope one day I find a folk story where all is not well under such circumstances). In the fullness of time – that is to say, a few years ago – it became necessary to widen the medieval bridge to take the holiday traffic. Borings showed all the piers to be founded on solid bed-rock. The truth of the story is that Lovibond paid for the building from a grant of tolls on bales of wool passing over it. This is an example of a frequent process. A folk story is generated by over literal interpretation of a metaphor. Revelation in a dream is common to much folklore.

Oral history. Collecting oral history from old people is a highly skilled speciality. Old people are not likely to talk into a tape recorder for anyone unless they trust them deeply. Yet when the tapes of an expert in this field, like George Ewart Evans,[†] are played, one realises just how much material there is to be recorded that will be irretrievably lost unless it is put on tape in the next few years.

This source can easily be undervalued by more traditional social historians. Mr Evans has showed how it can often make a unique contribution to our knowledge. For instance, by collecting stories in Suffolk pubs he discovered a system of seasonal migration of Norfolk and Suffolk agricultural workers at the beginning of the century, between growing barley in East Anglia and malting it at Burton upon Trent. Until then we knew nothing of what had deeply affected the lives of many.

Written memories. Surprisingly often, some of the work of recording has been done for us. One of the by-products of universal literacy are biographies, or unpretentious memories written usually in old age. Much, much slighter than the work of Flora Thompson,[†] they nevertheless provide additional and unique fragments from the same quarry to help us build our picture of recent British social history. In the next village to where I live, an old man born in 1829 wrote his memories roughly in a notebook in 1905, and took us back to the days when as a boy he minded his uncle's pigs on the open fields after harvest. For him the greatest change in his long life was the Enclosure. In the village on the other side, a son of a small peasant family had written of the social changes brought about there at the time of his village's Enclosure, with some of the most eloquent pleas of the peasant's case to the landowners, and the most elegaic scenes from the old countryman's year, like Mayday celebrations from the lost world.

Personal diaries, curiously enough – and this impression may just be a freak of my own experience – seem less frequent than accounts written in tranquillity in old age. Farmers' working diaries containing accounts of crops and cultivations can be particularly helpful to the social and economic historian, giving some of the detail that in most places was last available for the high Middle Ages. One small farmer's diary that I know for the middle of the nineteenth century lists the heriots he collected as agent for several of the manors in the village. These ranged from half-a-crown in cash to the clock off the parlour mantelpiece. The personal diary is likely only to be found for a person of particular interest. It took something special in the first place to write it.

Photographs and drawings. Going back now possibly beyond memories are old photographs. Local photographers may still have old plates from the foundation of the business, and in a family business this may be a very long way back indeed. Prints from these, particularly in the form of slides, will arouse such interest that they are probably the best backing for a general appeal to borrow old photographs for copying before they are lost for ever. These can reveal local characters and past fashions, which will have a great local appeal, but they will also reveal something of the transformation in local transport, with the coming of the bicycle and, hard after it, the internal combustion engine. With any luck, too, they will show the revolution of the petrol and diesel motor on the farm.

Old prints and topographical drawings are worth hunting for the usually unexpected light they throw on the local past. The British Library has an enormous collection and can produce the special catalogue for consultation. County Record Offices are very likely to have photo-copies of some, and possibly to know also of collections of, say, eighteenth-century antiquarians like the much underrated Stukeley, or William Cole. Stukeley has left us what is our only evidence of so many vanished buildings, and Cole left sketches of church after church among his vast collection of transcripts of historical materials. Early in the investigation of any locality should come the examination of anything left by local antiquarians, or collected by those ranging more widely, like the Lysons[†] with their *Magna Britannia* (which unfortunately only got as far as Devon when proceeding alphabetically), or Carlisle's *Topographical dictionary*.

The parish chest. Twenty years ago, in many places, the prime source for local history would have been the collection of documents in the parish chest. In recent years more and more have been gathered into County Record Offices, but always leaving the current registers, frequently for the whole of the past century, in the church. Whatever else may have gone from the parish, these remain, and for the history of families still living locally they are essential, although a far smaller proportion of the population fall into the church's net than in earlier centuries.

But registers were far from being the principal contents of the parish chests before so much went to County Record Offices. Contents varied enormously from church to church: Churchwardens' Accounts, Vestry Minute Books, Surveyors' Accounts for the Highways and, especially important, the Overseers' Accounts dealing with the administration of the Poor Law. Among the latter quite often there remain copies of Settlement Certificates, Removal Orders, Bastardy Claims and sometimes, after 1744, copies of the examination of vagrants by the JPs. The latter are especially valuable in that they often give thumbnail biographies of the poorest members of the community at a time when no parish wanted to know them, but pushed them on so that the cost of maintaining them fell outside the parish bounds. These examinations can give a vivid portrayal of this cruel process, and bring to life some otherwise mute, inglorious Oliver Twist. There will be more in the Quarter Session Records. Associated

with the poor law documents may be indentures of apprenticeship for pauper children.

Among the contents of parish chests may very well be whole collections which should have passed on when the County Councils were set up and the Vestry lost many of its rights and duties. These may include Tithe and Enclosure Award Maps, Rate-Books, and Papers of Charities which are no longer considered ecclesiastical and are now administered by other bodies. But as well as all the official, or formerly official, papers, some parsons from time to time kept unofficial extra registers for general information or special purposes of their own. Thus there may be records of briefs – letters asking for collections for charitable purposes such as relief after loss by fire or capture by the Barbary pirates. A vicar of a neighbouring parish kept copies of his letters to the bishop and the bishop's wearied replies. He details every move (usually wrong ones) which he made in his long battle with the very vigorous local Nonconformists.

Some general registers contain regular comments on the weather, attempts to analyse the figures from the registers requested by the bishop, and Family Listings either as asked for by ecclesiastical authority or government – for instance, under the Militia Act. These latter can give family size, and a check on total population. Some of these general registers have developed into scholarly collections of materials towards the history of the parish. Glebe terriers may be with the rest of the contents of the chest or they may only survive in the diocesan copies. These vary very much in the quality of information they offer. In some we get the most detailed descriptions that we ever find for houses standing in the seventeenth century, even covering the outhouses with their structures and uses.

In the course of time, as incumbents grow old and are sometimes reluctant to retire, and as not all of them have the habits and skills for caring for archives without the facilities to do it professionally, confusion may have arisen, and parish chests become enriched by the drift into them of materials more properly belonging to the benefice than the parish. Among such, records and papers of tithe disputes can be particularly valuable. The best description that I know of how an open-field system worked is in a case prepared for such a dispute in the last century in a nearby parish. However, for all the stray finds like this in the parish chest, there is much more to be found in the Diocesan Archives, if they prove to be accessible.

If tithes were a serious concern of most parsons for a thousand years or so, so also was the conduct of agriculture in the parish, in which, for most of the same period, the parson was actively involved, cropping the glebe. So in the chest, as well as Enclosure Acts, Maps and Awards, which should have passed on, we may find manorial court and account rolls, field books, books of regulations for common land, collections of by-laws and so on.

Manorial records. Before the Reformation increased the importance in local government of the parish, with its officers and vestry meetings, the manorial machinery was the core of local control and administration, and still remained active and with quite extensive power for a long time, especially where land was involved. The centre of manorial government was to be found in its courts, and the most extensive records are the court rolls and account rolls (and some series survive from early in the thirteenth century). Unfortunately for the amateur, for the earlier centuries these will all be in abbreviated Latin and written in a fairly difficult, spiky hand. As time goes by more of these become easily accessible in editions brought out by local Record Societies. Where keen amateur local historians who have a little Latin can be persuaded to brush up their knowledge for the less demanding medieval form of that language, they should be given every encouragement. The early court rolls and accounts rolls are amazingly detailed, and surprisingly richer than the corresponding ones from the early modern period. Even if a single court roll or account roll has been printed, it will repay the effort to squeeze maximum significance from it.

Manor courts were administrative as well as judicial assemblies, so their rolls record things like the supervision of land transfer, the appointment of local officers, as well as quarrels, misdemeanours and petty crime. The account rolls will record and account for all the farming operations, together with all expenses, payments and receipts for the lord's demesne when it is being directly cultivated. This is often recorded in astonishing detail. Very occasionally the rough drafts which the *reeve* produced for the accountant survive.

These may list the quantity and price of grain sown on the demesne of the lord, selion by selion, in every field and furlong.

The most common quarrels are cases of debt, assault and trespass. Tasters of Bread and Ale are regularly appointed and as regularly fined for failing to perform their office. Brewers and bakers are reported and automatically fined if they have brewed and baked; village victuallers were assumed never to conform to legal standards. Some of these items may seem routine, some insignificant, but they may very well be the ones which will repay quantitative study. The single unexpected item has a habit of suddenly appearing with a breath of life when the slow process of working through great piles of rolls has become a burden.

Sometimes we see human life and society epitomised in a court roll entry. In 1334, the villeins of the village where I now live appeared to be evening scores with their former reeve, John Frerer. They presented him for stealing various small quantities of the lord's corn; for keeping a certain foreign woman in the lord's bakehouse at the lord's expense; and for paying Milsent, his concubine, by sending a cartload of the lord's turves to the house where she was staying in the next village but one.* In another case nearby in 1367 we hear of a peasant who, in spite of being a villein and whose property was therefore his lord's, was acting as a moneylender. Fourteen years before, he had lent twenty shillings of silver to John Pepys, another villein, for merchandising and taking profit. The capital and interest were being reclaimed on Pepys' death.** It is through the accumulation of small incidents like this that the real picture of medieval life emerges.

Maps in words. As well as court and account rolls, other important and shorter documents survive in many manorial archives. These tend to merge rather than to follow very set separate forms: extents, surveys, terriers and field-books. They were mentioned earlier as sources for the understanding of field systems. In addition there may be rentals and custumals. Custumals detail the labour rents and other payments due according to the customs of the particular manor. Rentals list the rent-paying tenants, usually with details

*J. R. Ravensdale *Liable to floods*, p. 52.
**F. M. Page *The estates of Crowland Abbey*, p. 172.

of their holding and the rent due. Very often these are drawn up listing the tenants in order as the rent collector would come upon them in turn as he walked around the village, down one side of each street and up the other. This can be very helpful in working out the settlement plan, but only a part of the tenantry are likely to be listed on a rental, because only some tenants will pay cash rents, and there may well be landowners other than the lord for whom the rental is drawn up, involved in the village. This can decrease the usefulness of some of our other sources.

The term 'terrier' tends to be applied to a list of all the land of one estate; the term 'field book' to a complete list of all the open-field land in the village.

What can be most helpful is when a field book treats the built up area as part of the field land, treating each messuage as a strip, and grouping these as furlongs according to the adjacent field. My own village has such field-books made in 1477 and 1549. The later ones omit the built-up area. Where there is the inclusion of the house plots in a field-book, the chances of being able to map the complete village at an early date are very high. The key to solving this rather indeterminate jigsaw in my own parish was the mention of the roads and lanes of the time, which effectively sectioned the zones. This gave me enough information to work out where everyone lived. Three quarters of the late-medieval property boundaries still remained.

10 Population

Domesday. One of the simplest but most persistent questions that beset the historian of any place is 'How big was it?' In England, with the Domesday Book, we have a source on which to base a reasonable guess at the population of most places as early as 1086. For London and Winchester we have to go to other sources, and fortunately this can be done. However, since the boundary with Scotland was further south than today, some of the northern English, as well as Scots and Welsh, escaped the Norman tax assessment, which is what Domesday still seems to have been. Again, some places that we know were settled before Domesday are not mentioned in it. Many of these were probably included in other settlements. But we still have vital information for the vast proportion of English towns, villages and lesser settlements. For practical work on the Domesday Book, there are modern translations with helpful scholarly introductions for most counties in the *Victoria County History*, or Phillimore's new series 'History from the Sources'† under the general editorship of John Morris. There are peculiar local problems in every county text in Domesday which are dealt with in these introductions, such as the identification of some of the places mentioned, and peculiar local terms, or worse still, common terms with peculiar local meanings. With these introductions and the translation into English, handling Domesday material is no longer as formidable as it once was.

The information in Domesday is the result of a partial attempt to standardise material which was drawn out in answer to questions put to the local inhabitants, and there was much local variation. In most areas the finished work arranges its information in each county under lists of the King's Tenants-in-Chief, 'the Holders of Lands' (those who held directly of the King and not through any intermediate lord). These were usually listed by Hundreds (the local governmental unit) under each Tenant-in-Chief's name. The term 'manor' was normally used as the final unit of estate management, but there were detached fragments called 'berewicks' or other special local terms. Very often more than one manor went to make up a village – and,

on the other hand, many farms or hamlets could constitute one manor.

Nevertheless, just as Domesday does not describe houses, neither does it tell us directly the number of people living anywhere. What it does give is the number of holders of land in the various social classes that existed, or that Norman lawyers thought could be considered to exist in each manor. We have reason to believe that there were more priests than are mentioned, and that probably the others were counted as villeins. Some priests may have been heads of families, but already most were celibate. Then many slaves are mentioned in Domesday, and we do not know whether they would have families.

Some of the Domesday information on values is given at three periods, 1066, 1086 and when granted to its Tenant-in-Chief. Sometimes a brief mention is made of some of the Saxons who once held it, but rarely do the Saxon numbers mentioned constitute a plausible measure of the previous number of Saxon families that lived there. Except under very special circumstances, such as may occur when a manor appears to have been, before the Conquest, in the hands of a group of Saxon freemen who had no lord except the king, we cannot really get back beyond 1086 in our estimates of population. But we must take care to avoid double counting. Do we count the mesne tenant (the tenant of the tenant-in-chief) as resident with a family? If a priest is mentioned, do we count him as celibate or head of family? Similarly, do the slaves, whom the Saxons appear to have been using as ploughmen, count as one or a family?

These queries mean that we shall end our calculations with alternative figures, a bracket rather than a number, a probable order of magnitude. To convert the possible figures for numbers of households to figures of population, we need a multiplier, the average household size. Recent work on the size of the average medieval household in England seems to be producing a rather higher figure than we once used, around five. So, if a village of several manors produces a sum total of 5 cottars plus 1 bordar plus 10 villeins plus 1 priest and 4 slaves, we get a probable population size somewhere in the order of 85 to 105. This is only the roughest and readiest of figures, an indication of probability rather than a measure. Yet Domesday is unique, and is a better source for trying to discover the population of England than anything thereafter until the Tudor period.

The Hundred Rolls. A similar enquiry in greater detail than the Domesday Commission produced in 1278–79 what has come to be known as the Hundred Rolls. Only a part of the country is covered by what is known to survive, but for local historians in those parts they provide a gold mine which is only now beginning to be worked. The counties covered are Bedfordshire, Buckinghamshire, Cambridgeshire, Huntingdonshire, Leicestershire, Oxfordshire and Warwickshire. Some Rolls for Coventry and Suffolk were discovered in recent years, so we may well get more.

Where these survive, although they are in surprising detail, they describe the property in each village in terms of land, tenants and rents, in a fashion that invites exactly parallel calculations of population to those performed on the Domesday Book, with a resulting picture of population trend which gives much more confidence than any attempt to measure global size.

The weakness of the Hundred Rolls as a source for population studies is that, as with Domesday, they very rarely give any indication of the landless wage-labourers. This weakens the virtue even of our calculation of the trend. Caution is further imposed on us by the fact that in some estates in the Hundred Rolls we get specific mention of landless labourers under such delightful names as 'anilepemen' and 'anilepewimen', and we know from other sources of the existence of living-in manorial servants, 'famuli'. We know, again from other sources, of villeins employing labour, and others who are very active in the land market. Social patterns and economic classes are so blurred in the light of the extra detail that is given in the Hundred Rolls, that we suspect the completeness of what we are given both in 1278–79 and 1086.

Tax returns. Population size for the rest of the Middle Ages is even more problematical. Tax returns, whether Lay Subsidies or Poll Taxes, each require their own special multiplier, allowing for unknowns like the proportion of evasion. When some have been shown to be copies of old lists, not brought up to date but passed off as new, there seems little reliance to be placed in them. The processes by which special multipliers are derived seem to be influenced principally by what the calculator thinks his calculation should reveal.

The medieval tax lists seem at their most erratic dealing with small settlements. For regional shifts in wealth they seem much more plausible. Tax figures seem to become much more reliable from the Subsidy of 1524. Many of the Hearth Tax figures from the seventeenth century are now in print. In specially lucky areas these may be helped out by the occasional census or family listing required by the bishop, as in the Compton Census.* Such documents may turn up in the parish chest or the Diocesan Archives. There may also be copies of family lists under the Militia Act, giving enough detail to calculate family size.

Parish registers. It is in this early modern period that parish registers may come into their own. As they come down to us registers are very variable. They began in 1538, but relatively few now start before the parchment copies made in 1598, although some go back, as they should in these copies, to 1558. Even where there is an early start and a reasonably complete survival, the Civil War and Commonwealth period are likely to have breaks. The government took over responsibility for registration in 1653, and appointed Civil 'Registers' who sometimes completely failed to do their job.

The use of parish registers has been transformed in the last generation, chiefly due to the work, in this country, of the Cambridge Group for the History of Population and Social Structure. Associated with the Group is the journal *Local Population Studies*[†] and the Local Population Studies Society. These can be extremely useful to the amateur working in relative isolation as they provide a means of getting and keeping in touch with recent work, and with others currently working on similar materials and with similar problems. They are a unique way of keeping up to date with the progress of modern developments in the field.

In using Anglican registers for statistical purposes

*The listing of parishes by Communicants and Dissenters in 1676. Named after the Bishop of London.

the beginner would be well advised to read *Introduction to Historical Demography*,[†] E. A. Wrigley (ed), both to become aware of the limitations of this source, and also so that the researcher has the opportunity of using standard procedures and forms to obtain full value from the possibility of direct comparison with the results of an army of workers in the field.

Aggregation and reconstitution. Two main approaches have been used to make parish registers talk about population and population change, aggregative analysis and family reconstitution. The first counts monthly totals for each event, baptism, marriage and burial, and enters these on standard forms which enable annual totals to be inserted for both calendar year and harvest year, and changes in the birth rate to be seen in terms of approximate conception dates. The immediate value of this method is that it enables possible relationships between population changes and factors like harvests and epidemics to be seen at once, and vital questions asked. Family reconstitution operates by extracting all the information in the registers and sorting it on to new forms that bring it together by families. Where there is a good run of complete registration, this method produces enough information for the sociologist to calculate all the rates he needs to understand what is happening to population at a given time and place. A good set of records reconstituted will point, for instance, to periods when family limitation was being practised. When it is happening, it is bound to show up in birth intervals.

For many amateur local historians family reconstitution may prove to be the Great Divide, the point at which they stop short of going further with quantitative methods. On the other hand, Alan Macfarlane[†] would extend the principle of reconstitution to take in all local information. All is not necessarily lost if the local historian decides to remain an amateur amongst the professional players. The simple aggregate sheets will yield useful suggestions as to whether population in a specific period is being controlled by famine, and will even suggest what kind of epidemic may be the cause of other periods of high mortality. When there is a national influenza epidemic and our curate is recorded in the burial register as being carried off by the 'sweating sickness' we many reasonably take it that the

'flu has hit our parish. It can be the unique and eccentric pieces of information which enliven the search. For instance, in a rough hand dated 1594 and signed Nicholas Nemo, but in a space among the entries for 1562, there appears in our register: 'Pope, the fox Will eate no grapes, and Whi, he can not git y^m; so at this towne thei loue inglish servis, becaus thei can haue none other, as apperith bi the candeilbeme & rodlofte, as I think: iudge you by me.' It is useful to know that our rood loft and screen survived as late as 1594, in the parish church where Queen Elizabeth's first archbishop had last been an incumbent.

If you are embarking on further work on parish registers, either aggregate analysis or family reconstitution, it is probably as well to use a set of standard forms which will make comparison with other people's studies easy.

Was the population ever controlled by 'crises of subsistence'? How far did emigration from the parish alleviate the pressure from natural increase? The simple process of plotting comparative graphs of the three kinds of event through all the period covered by a good set of registers, especially if the trend is smoothed by plotting running averages, can quickly give some idea of long term growth of the community, and of periods of different kinds of growth.

Seasonality studies of marriages can possibly, by contrast with neighbouring parishes, indicate something of the bias of the local economy towards pasture or towards arable. Seasonality of burials may help to identify diseases. But seasonality of baptisms may tell us little, other than that it sometimes seems to have been the local custom to defer baptisms until harvest could pay for the celebration and wetting the baby's head. Already in the eighteenth century one gets the impression from some families being baptised all together, that some were no longer being baptised at all, certainly not by the Anglican rite.

Windows into men's souls. Here, as we come on to the effect of religious differences, our material may make more subtle suggestions to us. Do absences of marriages from the register in Lent in the late sixteenth century indicate a strong survival of Catholic beliefs?

Such attempts to find windows into the souls of our humble forefathers seem destined to break down just as they seem near to success, but if any historian finds out how to know the faith and feelings of the ordinary Englishman of three or four centuries ago, it is likely to be a local historian.

The census. Anglican parish registers become less and less comprehensive with the rise of Nonconformity, and early in the nineteenth century, a generation or so before the coming of Civil Registration in 1837, they lose their reliability. The early censuses give very little information apart from numbers, but from 1851 the rate of survival is very good, and the recorded information very wide. Many county archivists have collected microfilm of the enumerators' notebooks for their county for the censuses of 1851, 1861 and 1871, and will add to this as each new census becomes available under the hundred-year rule of confidentiality. The 1851 books give, household by household, the name, state, age, sex, occupation, relation to head of household and parish of origin of each resident. They also note the number of houses occupied, unoccupied and building. Much fascinating work can be done on these, either on single parishes or groups of parishes. To get full value from these returns, the local historian often has a very difficult puzzle to start with, the indentification of houses by the enumerators' numbers. A few luckily placed farmhouses, blacksmiths' shops or public houses may help to relate 1851 households to the modern map, but it is not always clear what the enumerator is counting as a house or household. Where two families live in one house, he often seems to count this not only as two households but as two houses as well.

In spite of this, the availability of such a splendid source as the 1851 census makes that year an admirable point at which to begin the study of the history of any place. From such a base one can move forward or back in time. This was the procedure recommended in that excellent guide for local history groups, *This was their world*, by Alan Rogers (or, in its revised edition, *Approaches to local history*[†]).

It was in association with the census enquiry of that year that the so-called religious census was taken, and unreliable as are the voluntary returns made about the state of religious practice, they are all we have.

However, probably one of the best ways in which to begin a local study from census materials in a very simple way is to take the printed census totals and plot them in order as a graph for each parish in the chosen area from 1801. The easiest place to get these figures is probably the *Victoria County History*, which prints them in tabulated form with notes to explain accidental discrepancies, such as the return of natives for the village feast, with the consequent inflation of that year's figures. In urban areas this enables the outline of the development of the town to be seen at once, with old built-up areas stationary or falling, and the parishes where the new development is filling up with speed. In both town and country there will be divergencies in the pattern of growth with groups emerging of one kind distinct from that followed by others. Even for what is intended to be, a rural study, it is important to produce comparable graphs for urban parishes. If we come across a drift from the countryside, we should like to know how far the migrants are absorbed by growing local towns. The places of origin in the 1851 census will enable another side of migration to be seen, and something like a radius of courtship for the humbler social classes to be measured.

If we wish to follow migration further in time, our capacity to do so in the early modern period depends on how informative our records are in recording places of origin of brides and grooms. This cannot merely vary from parish to parish, but also from parson to parson, and even according to age or infirmity during each incumbency.

11 More Recent Years

Newspapers. Many local historians are not yet making as much use of local newspapers as they should. If newspapers' bulk represents a real difficulty, their richness more than compensates. At one time or other most parts of the country will have been covered by several papers, some of them running back to the eighteenth century. After the middle of the nineteenth century a mushroom growth of small newspapers should have added more to the archives.

To exploit them thoroughly takes a great deal of time, and the student has to learn to resist a very natural urge to start reading quite irrelevant material. It is the same urge that one feels while wrapping crockery when moving house. One cannot afford to waste any time when working on newspapers if much travelling is involved. The greatest possible saver of time is an index, and the Cambridgeshire local library collection, for example, is well on with the work of indexing its newspapers. We found that the Ealing Borough Library's index made it possible to study Middlesex papers despite the shortage of time.

Another way of saving time I discovered in Cornwall. In Liskeard I had easy access to a set of files of the *Cornish Times*, a local weekly founded in 1857. The main daily newspapers could only be seen a long way away in Plymouth or Truro, and to work on them would have involved more expense and time than could be justified. But the *Cornish Times*, like many of its contemporaries, consisted of one sheet folded in four. One side of the open sheet was printed in London, with national news and advertisements. The other half was printed in Cornwall, with Cornish news and advertisement. The result of this was that there was a very terse weekly summary of the news, which could be very quickly scanned. Where more detail was required, a note with the date meant that the long distance work now only needed a manageable amount of time. The total time needed was drastically reduced, and the actual process of searching more effective. I can certainly recommend such little weeklies. They also have the advantage that, with space at such a premium, the reporting tended to be excellent.

There were other consequences of the size of the *Cornish Times*. Week by week it printed tabulated changes in mineral prices and mining shares, and international intelligence on minerals. This was the period of dramatic collapses in copper and tin, and the rise of china clay. It was the age of the Great Depression in Cornish agriculture and mining (whether or not historians will allow such for the rest of the country and the rest of industry). The little weekly paper was also in effect a local *Economist*. The background of the diaspora of Cornish Miners was never absent, and the advertisement columns were much occupied with emigrant ships offering passages to wherever there was metal ore in rock. Letters home, some of which may have been imaginary, were inserted as further advertisement for new worlds. But the news of the strikes in the coalfields that the Cornish miners had gone to break unwittingly, were conscientiously reported, as were the strikes by the Cornishmen when they found out how they had been used. It is most unlikely that our descendants will be served by our local papers as well as we are by those of our Victorian forebears. Their sense of fairness was as acute as their sensitivity to language.

Blue Books. A good, rich source for expanding and strengthening nineteenth-century history in any locality is the Blue Books or Parliamentary Papers. Especially valuable are the Minutes of Evidence before the major commissions. The local historian will need to discover material of particular relevance to his own proper subject by searching indexes. Initially he should consult the Historical Association pamphlet, *Local history from Blue books: a select list of the sessional Papers of the House of Commons*, by W. R. Powell. Some of these may have become more easily accessible since the Irish Universities Press began reprinting Blue Books. A new development for improved accessibility is the publication in microfiche on behalf of the Consortium of British Libraries by Chadwyck-Healey Ltd, of the *House of Commons Parliamentary Papers, 1801–1900*. However, even some thirty years ago the county librarian was able to borrow Parliamentary

Papers for me through the national inter-library borrowing scheme.

Blue Books are particularly plentiful in local material in topics such as charities, the poor and the Poor Law, agriculture and employment in it, distress in agriculture, depression in industry and trade, labour relations and education. The student must make his way with the help of indexes and where there are none, by tables of contents and contents headings.

Education. Education is particularly well supplied by records, and this is most fortunate, since it arouses so much interest as a subject for local historians. The quantity of material from the nineteenth century on education is such that all the fascinating educational history from earlier centuries is merely the *hors d'oeuvre*. Even in the latest period, with so many impressive national reports, an enormous amount of relevant material is in the County Record Offices, and a great deal seems to have escaped the repositories and is still in local hands. With the closure of so many small schools, especially with the fall in the birth-rate of recent years, papers that could have been invaluable to the historian have been dispersed, and even worse possibly destroyed.

If one wants to discover how a village came to lose its school, which may well have been the major social institution there, as well as much else, a good set of Managers' Minutes will tell a great deal, but will probably miss most of the drama unless they are supplemented by press reports. It can come as a revelation to discover how long the rearguard action against closure went on, or how fatuous the official reasons for closure were. Similarly, the irrational may be the key to the story of the treatment of some voluntary schools when they were making their ways into the state system after 1870.

Since the Second World War most school log-books have found their way into the hands of county archivists. These can both be very informative and highly amusing. I remember one such where an irate HMI's scrawl ran diagonally across two pages of a log-book. He had arrived at a remote moorland school, to find that the headmaster was twenty miles away in the nearest town, performing his duties as Clerk to the Guardians, leaving the school in charge of his wife and daughter. The big boys were lighting sticks in the fire, and chasing the girls with them. Every stroke of the Inspector's pen suggested that the sky was about to fall, but the same headmaster's hand resumed on the next page and continued for years.

Log-books can be full of information on social conditions of the time. Epidemics, absences in fruit- and potato-picking seasons, and the head's view on them occur again and again. One note on the educational difficulties of a Gipsy family described an annual triangular pattern of travelling that a Gipsy family of the same name were following as long as seventy years later.

This is also an area where oral history has a great part to play. There must be many who can just remember teachers whose careers went back to the 1870 Act, but they are growing fewer rapidly. Old men's memories seem particularly active when recalling early school-days, and even more so in recounting tales of early teachers. When two or three near-contemporaries are gathered together, the flow of recollections is greater and steadier. The presence of other witnesses can often curb fantasy.

12 Industrial Archaeology

Industrial archaeology became a self-conscious separate subject, almost as an offshoot of the surging interest in landscape history in the mid-1950s. Local historians awoke and realised that they had been speaking prose – industrial archaeology – all their lives. History has obviously a great deal to borrow from industrial archaeology, and it is only fitting that this country, where the first industrial society was built and so many of the first crucial inventions were made, should preserve remaining monuments of the industries that once led the world.

There is so much remaining from early industries that deserves recording or preserving that is is difficult to know where to start and where to stop. There is so much need for the collecting of information and artefacts, and setting up and filling still more museums, that collecting industrial junk, with or without the aid of metal detectors, has become a swollen adjunct of the new subject. Train-spotting and the collection of Victoriana were already operating in the field when the new subject was born. The collection of objects such as cast-iron drain covers, or of post boxes, may have corresponded to grave-robbing as a phase in the prehistory of classical archaeology.

Yet very exciting things have happened. The actual hearths used by the Darby family at Coalbrookdale in their critical achievements in smelting, with the original names and dates, were discovered *in situ*, and their works restored as one of the best industrial museums. The individual items of plant and equipment on display are artefacts from the fount of one great phase of the Industrial Revolution. The lay-out of the whole complex suggested the logic of the relation between sources of raw material – iron ore and coal, and water transport – the outlet for heavy, bulk products. However, the accounts showed that its operation was much more clumsy and illogical, at times at least, and far from efficient.*

What is happening in a display such as this is that the multi-disciplinary approach is showing its benefits,

where each discipline can add its correcting contribution, flashing a warning light if offered too simple an answer. We learned more industrial history as the object of examination widened from the particular (a few yards of rail-track) to the operation and relation of all that had come together in that enterprise. Obviously a new industrial history will grow as the industrial archaeologist works out his full contribution to a set of central themes. His relation to this new industrial history will only partly correspond to the relationship between the prehistoric archaeologist and prehistory, because the industrial archaeologist will have to meet the simultaneous requirements of the historian, who will be breathing down his neck.

The local historian is unlikely to be more than an assistant to the local industrial archaeologist, but perhaps a more useful assistant to him than he is to the local prehistoric archaeologist, simply because he works with documents which refer to the industrial archaeologist's artefacts, and because both will often be studying the same society. Each has much to offer the other, to help make understanding more complete. The chances that an industrial archaeologist may be able to study much wider local history outside his specialism is remote: care and preservation of industrial monuments can become an all-absorbing task.

On a walk right across Bodmin Moor to the north-east, however, starting from the point where Cornish hills almost become mountains, it is easy to see the connection between industrial archaeology and the investigation of man's past by other means, historical or archaeological. On the south-western slopes of Rough-tor are spread out the huts and compounds of what looks to have been the Black Country of the Early Bronze Age. A settlement of this size immediately above the marshy ground covering the tin-bearing gravels at this period must rank it as one of our more important prehistoric industrial sites. And this area, and the moorland spreading out from it, remained an industrial site almost ever after. On the north-east corner of the granite mass that forms the moor, the last of the old beam-engine mines only stopped working in

*Barrie Trinder, *Industrial archaeology* in *Landscape and documents*, edited by Alan Rogers and Trevor Rowley. Bedford Press, 1974.

living memory. In between, tin-streaming appears to have shut down in the later Bronze Age, but to have reopened in the Iron Age and to have continued, except for a gap in the Dark Ages, to beyond the Domesday survey. In the Middle Ages documentary and archaeological evidence join up to reveal tin-working on the moor, and continue into the twenties and thirties of this century. All across the moor are stream-workings, costain (trial) pits, rows of shallow pits where the 'old men' worked the back of a lode, deep shafts fenced around with barbed wire and the remains of engine houses.

A photograph from the 1880s of Phoenix mine shows no less than eight engine houses in the one view, and down below were water-wheels, some of them enormous, transmitting their power to where it was wanted by flat-rods. Launders carried water from the other side of the valley. Activity and energy were concentrated in what must have been a din that is amazing to anyone who sees the valley now, almost deserted, where the voice of the boy calling to his dog carries from a mile away. The remains of virtually all the mining processes are still here.

A large part of industrial archaeology goes beyond the nuts and bolts of mechanical processes, and examines not only the 'dark satanic mills' and their engines, but also the houses and the living conditions of those who worked the factories. 'Each chartered street' too, has its own proper story.

One of the most elegant small masterpieces of English landscape history is Professor Beresford's Inaugural Lecture at Leeds, *Time and Place*.[*] In it he staked once more the claim of the English landscape as evidence for English economic and social history, and gave an example of how best to use landscape evidence. The streets of Leeds first revealed their pattern to him by showing booms and slumps of the nineteenth century. The small, often odd-shaped blocks of development by speculators preserved the old field shapes as the lots fell to the developers. Beyond this, clues in the lay-out pointed back to still earlier medieval fields, and the planned medieval town which was added to the village, in its turn older still.

It is perhaps fitting that our exploration should have brought us, thus, full circle. We started with a village which turned out to have been a planned medieval town, and we end with an industrial town which appears to be a complete contrast to our village, and yet it, too, had passed through the stages of medieval village and planned town. When I first became interested we could have seen none of this. Now thanks to Professor Hoskins, Professor Beresford, Christopher Taylor, and the rest of those who have worked in the field for the past twenty-five years, we can not only arrive back home and know the place for the first time; we can have the sheer delight of exploring and finding local history everywhere in the English landscape.

[*]M. W. Beresford *Time and place, an inaugural lecture*. Leeds University Press, 1961.

Glossary

acre A unit of land either customary or measured. The customary acre was the amount a plough team would plough in a day and was visible as the ridge in the fields. The measured acre was standardised by Edward I as 220 × 22 yds. (The customary acre was rarely more than $\frac{2}{3}$ of measured acre).

baulk An access way between furlongs and strips in the Open Field.

burgess A town dweller who holds his house and land by a special form of free tenure.

butt A truncated selion.

chancery A Royal Prerogative Court of very ancient origins to which many local cases went. Its records are calendared in Letters Patent, Close Rolls and Charter Rolls. They detail, among other things, grants of land and privileges, enclosure awards and investigations as to market and fair rights.

clerestory A wall containing windows above the aisle arcade.

croft A small enclosure of land, sometimes behind a toft (qv) and associated with it.

demesne The part of the Manor held in the Lord's hand and cultivated for his use.

Easter sepulchre A shallow recess with a bench or tomb chest in the North wall of nave or chancel, which played a central role in the Easter liturgy, holding the host consecrated in the last Mass before Easter until first Mass of Easter day. Vigil was kept over it by two women representing Martha and Mary.

extent A written description of land – Manor or estate – otherwise known as a survey or terrier.

field Arable land in a large topographical unit and often the unit of rotation.

furlong As a unit of length – 22 yards. As a unit of area it is a bundle of selions (qv) all running in the same direction.

furrow The groove made by a plough in the soil or the hollow between two plough ridges.

gore A triangular piece of ploughed land in an awkward corner of the Open Field.

headland A piece of land running across the end of a bunch of selions – where the plough team turned.

hide A measure of land. A standard 120 acres or local customary variant.

house platform The low rectangular mound that marks the ruined foundations of medieval peasant houses.

impost moulding Moulding at the point from which an arch springs.

inquisition The process or record of information obtained by questions put to a sworn jury.

jetty The overhang (oversailing) of the upper storey of a timber framed house jutting over the lower floor.

knight's fee Land held of the King in return for say, 40 days service of a fully armed and equipped Knight per year.

lammas land Land open to common grazing on Lammas Day, 1st August – especially used for meadow land after hay has been taken off.

leat An artificial watercourse which diverts water from a river or stream to a watermill.

lode A watercourse normally used for carrying barges.

manor A unit of estate management usually with a principal house. The holder is known as Lord of the Manor, and as such has various rights over land and tenants. The parish could contain several manors or a manor could embrace more than one parish.

pannage The right to feed swine in woodlands.

piscina Stone basin and drain set in the wall by an altar, for washing chalice and patten after Mass.

quoin The brick or stone corners of a building.

reeve The local supervisor held responsible for the running of a Manor.

ridge The unit of land ploughed by a team in a day.

sedilia Stone seats for the priests (usually three) on the south side of the chancel of a church.

selion see ridge.

Star Chamber A Royal Prerogative Court which dealt with cases involving violence.

straight joint Arrangement of courses in building so that joints between stones come vertically above each other and make wall weak at this point.

string course A horizontal projection of stone set in a surface of wall and often with mouldings or shapes very characteristic of the building style.

strip The unit of land tenure which consists of one or more selions or ridges in the open fields (a modern term) or a strip of meadow marked out for mowing.

terrier See extent.

toft An enclosure in which a peasant's house stands or stood.

villein An unfree tenant, not a slave, treated as the property of his lord. The test of villeinage is week work, the duty of giving regular weekly labour to his lord in return for his landowning.

virgate A measure of land – $\frac{1}{4}$ of a hide – either the standard 30 acres or some local customary variant. The normal villein holding is a virgate or $\frac{1}{2}$ virgate.

week work Labour required by the lord of the manor of a villein, every week of the year on a specified weekday or days, in return for the villein holding land.

Bibliography

Introduction

HOSKINS, W. G. *The making of the English landscape* Hodder and Stoughton, rev. edn. 1977; Penguin Books, 1970. Essential reading for pleasure, and the foundation of a new and fruitful approach to local history.

A series of county volumes has been published by Hodder and Stoughton and more are coming out:

ALLISON, K. J. *The East Riding of Yorkshire* 1976.

BALCHIN, W. G. V. *Cornwall* 1955.

BIGMORE, P. *The Bedfordshire and Huntingdonshire landscape* 1979.

BRANDON, P. *The Sussex landscape* 1974.

DYMOND, D. *The Norfolk landscape* due 1982.

EMERY, F. V. *The Oxfordshire landscape* 1974.

FINBERG, H. P. R. *Gloucestershire* n.e. 1975.

HAVINDEN, M. *The Somerset landscape* n.y.p.

HOSKINS, W. G. *Leicestershire* 1957. op.

MILLWARD, R. *Lancashire* 1955.

MUNBY, L. M. *Hertfordshire* 1977.

NEWTON, R. *The Northumberland landscape* 1972.

PALLISER, D. M. *The Staffordshire landscape* 1976.

RAISTRICK, A. *The West Riding of Yorkshire* 1970.

REED, M. *The Buckinghamshire landscape* 1979.

ROWLEY, T. *The Shropshire landscape* 1972.

SCARFE, N. *Suffolk* 1972.

STEANE, J. M. *The Northamptonshire landscape* 1974.

TAYLOR, C. *The Cambridgeshire landscape* 1973.

TAYLOR, C. *The Dorset landscape* 1970.

ASHBY, M. K. *The changing English village* Roundwood Press, 1974. A model village study.

DARBY, H. C. *A new historical geography of England before 1600* CUP, n.e. 1978; paperback 1976. Sets some of the themes that the local historian takes up.

DYMOND, D. P. *Writing local history: a practical guide* Bedford Square Press: Macdonald and Evans, 1981. The best thing yet written on the subject.

GOUGH, R. *The history of Myddle* Firle: Caliban Books, 1979; Penguin Books, 1981. An amazing village history written in the seventeenth century, that we can enjoy but never hope to emulate.

IREDALE, D. *Enjoying archives* David and Charles, 1973.

IREDALE, D. *Discovering local history* Shire Publications, n.e. 1980.

IREDALE, D. *Discovering your old house* Shire Publications, n.e. 1980.

IREDALE, D. *Discovering your family tree* Shire Publications, n.e. 1980. A series of very useful, simple and practical pamphlets. Each will make an excellent start to an investigation.

JOSSELIN, R. *The diary of Ralph Josselin, 1616–1683* ed. by A. D. J. Macfarlane. OUP, 1976.

MACFARLANE, A. D. J. *The family life of Ralph Josselin* CUP, 1970

MACFARLANE, A. D. J. *Reconstructing historical communities* CUP, 1977. A series of local studies, based on the complete exploitation of a very full set of village records and a remarkable parson's diary from the seventeenth century. The ultimate in techniques for making local studies complete.

MUIR, R. *The English village* Thames and Hudson, 1980. A rare combination of elegant writing, sound history and superb photography.

MUIR, R. *The Shell guide to reading the landscape* M. Joseph, 1981. A complete course in landscape history.

PARKER, R. *The common stream: Foxton* Collins 1975 op; Paladin, 1976. The quest for the history of a house and a village. Delightful reading.

PARKER, R. *Cottage on the green* Research Publishing Co., 1973. op.

POSTAN, M. M. *The medieval economy and society: economic history of Britain, 1100–1500* Weidenfeld and Nicolson, 1972; Penguin Books, 1975. A clear outline of the shape into which any local medieval social and economic study has to fit.

RACKHAM, O. *Trees and woodland in the British landscape* Dent, 1976. A masterly work from which we can all learn much

RICHARDSON, J. *The local historian's encyclopaedia* 1974. Historical Publications, Orchard House, 54 Station Rd., New Barnet, Herts. Probably the most useful book for the working local historian that has ever been published. A copy should always be kept at hand.

ROGERS, A. *Approaches to local history* 2nd revised edn. of *This was their world* Longman, 1977. Some well worked out schemes for investigating modern local history, especially useful for setting up group projects.

ROWLEY, T. *Villages in the landscape* Dent, 1978. An example of the work of a writer who is repeatedly developing the subject of local studies.

SPUFFORD, M. *Contrasting communities: English villagers in the sixteenth and seventeenth centuries* CUP, 1974; n.e. paperback 1979. A work of art which carried the study of local history forward to new achievements.

STEPHENS, W. B. *Sources for English local history* Manchester University Press, 1972. op; CUP rev. edn, 1981. This is by far the best book on the sources that the local historian can use.

TINDALL, G. *The fields beneath : the history of one London village* M. Temple Smith, 1977; Paladin, 1980. An example of the richness that awaits the local historian in London suburbs.

Chapter One

BERESFORD, M. W. *New towns of the middle ages* Lutterworth Press, 1967. op. A very important seminal book, which is still a pleasure to read.

FARRER, W. *Feudal Cambridgeshire* CUP, 1920.

The Record Commission *Rotuli Hundredorum* 1812 and 1818.

The Victoria history of the counties of England HMSO various. These volumes are being published as ready in a series for each county. If some are old-fashioned by now no local historian can afford to ignore them.

Chapter Two

CORNWALL, J. *How to read old title deeds, xvi–xix centuries* University of Birmingham, Department of Extramural Studies, 1964. op; Pinhorns, n.i. 1970.

Chapter Three

Fieldwork

All the books below give examples of the kind of fieldwork that the local historian uses today.

ASTON, M. and ROWLEY, T. *Landscape archaeology* David and Charles, 1974.

BERESFORD, M. W. *History on the ground : six studies in maps and landscapes* Methuen, rev. edn. 1971.

BERESFORD, M. W. and ST JOSEPH, J. K. *Medieval England : an aerial survey* CUP, 2nd edn. 1979.

CRAWFORD, O. G. S. *Archaeology in the field* Phoenix House, 1953. op.

DYER, J. *Discovering archaeology in England and Wales* Shire Publications, n.e. 1976.

HOSKINS, W. G. *Fieldwork in local history* Faber, 1969. op.

TAYLOR, C. *Fieldwork in mediaeval archaeology* Batsford, 1975.

Maps and boundaries

BERESFORD, M. W. *History on the ground : six studies in maps and landscapes* Methuen, n.e. 1971. This is one of the books that showed the possibility of reading history from maps that Maitland and Hoskins had attempted earlier.

These two pamphlets enable historians to exploit the whole range of surviving maps; two most valuable handlists:

HARLEY, J. B. *Maps for the local historian : a guide to the British sources* National Council for Voluntary Organisations, 1972.

HARLEY, J. B. and PHILLIPS, C. W. *The historian's guide to Ordnance Survey maps* NCVO. 1965. op. reprinting.

Chapter Four

ASTON, M. and BOND, J. C. *Landscape of towns* Dent, 1976. The latest work that breaks new ground.

FINBERG, J. *Exploring villages* Routledge and Kegan Paul, 1958. op. An old friend for beginners.

Chapter Five

BAKER, A. R. H. and HARLEY, J. B. eds. *Man made the land* David and Charles, 1973. A collection of articles that very neatly summarise recent work of especial importance for the local historian.

BAKER, A. R. H. and BUTLIN, R. A. eds. *Studies of field systems in the British Isles* CUP, 1973; n.e. paperback 1980. A most helpful guide in showing local variations, and so aiding the assessment of the significance of the findings in any area.

BERESFORD, M. W. and HURST, J. G. *Deserted medieval villages* Lutterworth Press, 1971. Very valuable at the point where archaeological evidence has to supply all that we know about vanished medieval peasant houses.

BOWEN, H. C. *Ancient fields* BAAS 1962. op; S. R. Publications, 1970. Still one of the clearest outlines of this subject.

BOWEN, H. C. and FOWLER, P. J. *Early land allotment in the British Isles* British Archaeological Reports, 1978.

FISHER, J. L. *A medieval farming glossary of Latin and English words* NCVO, 1968. A very remarkable collection which very often supplies an answer when much larger books fail.

KERRIDGE, E. *The agricultural revolution* Allen and Unwin 1967. op; Kelley, USA, 1977. Essential reading for anyone writing a general local history.

ORWIN, C. S. and C. S. *The open fields* OUP 3rd edn. ed. Joan Thirsk. 1967. op. Great pioneer work. May need revision.

TATE, W. E. *The English village community and the enclosure movements* Gollancz, 1967. Full of practical details of the process of enclosure and of what may survive in the way of significant records.

TAYLOR, C. C. *Fields in the English landscape* Dent, 1975. The author's experience and knowledge in this area is unrivalled. This book requires careful study by all local historians.

Chapter Six

BARLEY, M. W. *The English farmhouse and cottage* Routledge and Kegan Paul, 1961. Full of material, although the line of argument may need revision.

BRUNSKILL, R. W. *The illustrated handbook of vernacular architecture* Faber, n.e. cased and paperback 1978. An excellent hand-book.

CLIFTON-TAYLOR, A. *The pattern of English building* Faber, 1972.

EDEN, P. 'Smaller post-medieval houses in eastern England' in *East Anglian studies* edited by L. M. Munby. Cambridge: Heffer, 1968. Probably still one of the most important articles on this subject.

IREDALE, D. *Discovering your old house* Shire Publications, n.e. 1980.

PARKER, V. *The English house in the nineteenth century* Historical Association, 1970. A very clear outline.

PEVSNER, N. ed. *The buildings of England* by counties, Penguin Books, cased and paperback. The first handbook of local buildings anywhere in the country.

ROYAL COMMISSION ON HISTORICAL MONUMENTS *English vernacular houses: a study of traditional farm houses and cottages* HMSO, 1975. This is an attempt at synthesising all current knowledge on the subject: essential reading.

Chapter Seven

Two recent important research reports among many on parish churches, published by the Council for British Archaeology.

COUNCIL FOR BRITISH ARCHAEOLOGY *The archaeological study of churches*, 1976.

COUNCIL FOR BRITISH ARCHAEOLOGY *Historic churches: a wasting asset*, 1977.

FOSTER, R. *Discovering English churches*, BBC, 1981.

TAYLOR, H. and J. *Anglo Saxon architecture* CUP, 3 vols. 1965–78.

Chapter Nine

The first two books below are invaluable to the local historian.

EKWALL, E. *The concise Oxford dictionary of English place-names* Clarendon Press, 4th edn. 1960.

THE ENGLISH PLACE-NAME SOCIETY *The place-names of . . .* county volumes.

HECTOR, L. C. *The hand-writing of English documents* Edward Arnold, n.e. 1966; Dorking: Kohler and Coombes, 1980. A very thorough and helpful explanation and handbook.

LATHAM, R. E. *Revised medieval Latin word-list* OUP, 1965. The standard very necessary work.

MARTIN, C. T. *The record interpreter* 1892. Dorking: Kohler and Coombes, facsim. of 1910 edn. 1976. Full of information helpful to those reading original sources.

SMITH, A. H. *English place-name elements* CUP for EPNS, n.e. 2 vols. 1971. An essential aid for any attempt to make original interpretations of the meaning of place-names.

STEEL, D. *Discovering your family history* BBC, cased and paperback, 1980. The complete handbook and instructions on how to do it, and an enthralling tale of the pursuit of family history.

TATE, W. E. *The parish chest: a study of the records of parochial administration in England* CUP, 3rd edn. 1969. A guide to the most used source, whose popularity and use have increased yearly.

THOMPSON, P. *The voice of the past: oral history* OUP, 1978. Discusses something of the philosophy as well as techniques.

Chapter Ten

GIBSON, J. S. W. *Wills and where to find them* Phillimore, 1974. Extremely useful.

STEER, F. W. *Farm and cottage inventories of mid-Essex, 1635–1749* Phillimore 1969. An excellent introduction to this prolific and informative source.

WRIGLEY, E. A. *Population and history* Weidenfeld and Nicolson, 1969.

WRIGLEY, E. A. ed. *An introduction to English historical demography: from the sixteenth to the nineteenth century* Weidenfeld and Nicolson, 1966. op. Introductions to the practice and implications of the study of population in history by a master.

Chapter Eleven

CAMP, A. J. *Wills and their whereabouts* the Author, 1974 (c/o the Society of Genealogists). Helpful in breaking into an important source for local social history.

Three books designed to suit the amateur by one of our most eminent archivists:

EMMISON, F. G. *Archives and local history* Phillimore, n.e. 1978.

EMMISON, F. G. *How to read local archives, 1550–1700* Historical Association, n.e. 1980.

EMMISON, F. G. *Introduction to archives* Phillimore, n.e. 1978.

EVANS, G. E. *Ask the fellow who cut the hay* Faber, 1956.

EVANS, G. E. *Horse power and magic* Faber, 1979.

All the books of this delightful writer should be read by the student before embarking on writing on his own account. They are masterpieces in the recovery of a lost world.

GOODER, E. A. *Latin for local history* Longman, n.e. 1978. This has helped many students to acquire competence sufficient for handling medieval records.

GRIEVE, H. *Examples of English handwriting, 1150–1750* Essex Record Office, 2nd edn. 1959. A good choice of facsimiles for practice reading.

OWEN, D. M. *The records of the established church in England excluding parochial records* British Records Association, 1970. An essential guide for entry to one of the largest and most important groups of documents.

Chapter Twelve

BERESFORD, M. W. *Time and place: an inaugural lecture* Leeds University Press, 1961. An elegant and remarkable use of visual evidence in a survey ranging through the whole history of Leeds.

BRIGGS, A. *Victorian cities* Odhams, 1963. op; Penguin Books, 1968. Essential reading for any person studying a nineteenth-century industrial city.

BUCHANAN, R. A. *Industrial archaeology in Britain* Penguin Books, 1972. An outline of the whole subject.

BURTON, A. *The past at work* BBC: Deutsch, 1980. An outline with outstanding photographs.

DYOS, H. J. *Victorian suburb: study of the growth of Camberwell* Leicester University Press, 1973. The complete model of how to tackle suburban history.

Periodicals

There are two of particular relevance to local historians:

The Local Historian quarterly. National Council for Voluntary Organisations, 26 Bedford Square, London WC1B 3HU. This is a means of breaking down the isolation in which a local historian can find himself. It enables the reader to sample what other people are doing and to pick up and share new methods as they are introduced. All serious local historians should subscribe.

Local Population Studies a more specialised magazine, but with only two issues per year. Any student of local population would be well advised to read this, and might well consider joining the Local Population Studies Society. The Subscription secretary of the society is Mrs M. H. Charlton, 9 Lisburne Square, Torquay, Devon.

Index